Writing and Thinking with Computers

Writing and Thinking with Computers

A Practical and Progressive Approach

Rick Monroe
Woodinville High School
Woodinville, Washington

National Council of Teachers of English
1111 W. Kenyon Road, Urbana, Illinois 61801-1096

Dedicated to Marie for her love and friendship.

Manuscript Editor: Mary C. Graham

Production Editors: William Tucker and Rona S. Smith

Cover Design: Carlton Bruett

Interior Design: Doug Burnett

NCTE Stock Number 58935-3050

Library of Congress Cataloging-in-Publication Data

Monroe, Rick, 1954–
  Writing and thinking with computers : a practical and
progressive approach / Rick Monroe.
     p.   cm.
  Includes bibliographical references.
  ISBN 0-8141-5893-5
  1. English language—Composition and exercises—Computer-assisted instruction.   2. English language—Composition and exercises—Study and teaching (Secondary)   3. Critical thinking—Computer-assisted instruction.   4. Critical thinking—Study and teaching (Secondary)
I. Title.
PE1404.M66   1993
808'.042'0285416—dc20   93-1474
                                                                  CIP

Contents

Acknowledgments   ix

Preface   xi

Introduction   xiii

    A Philosophical Stance   xiii

    The Rationale for an Application-Based
    Computer Curriculum   xv

1. Computers in the Classroom   1

    Motivating Students to Write   2

    Electronic Read-Arounds and Other
    Computer-Writing Strategies   4

    More about Lesson Files and Shared Folders   11

    More about Modeling   19

    Imitation and the Split Screen   24

    "What If" and the Business Letter   26

    Drawing into Narrative   30

    Making Connections with Clip Art   32

    Writing and Responding to Literature   33

    Extending Student Writing: The Year-End Book   44

    Restructuring the Classroom for Technology   46

    Evaluating Student Writing Equitably and Efficiently   49

    Additional Thoughts   54

2. Establishing a Networked Computer Lab   61

    The Basics   61

    Managing a Local Area Network   64

    Access Privileges and Sample Log-On Procedures 70

Planning for Success   72

Introduction to Word Processing   76

3. **Extending the Uses of Technology**   83

Imagining and Making the Future   83

Publishing Student Work Using Desktop Publishing   91

Telecommunications: A Primer   94

Book Reviews with FileMaker Pro   97

4. **Using Computers across Disciplines**   102

Sample Lesson 1: Math Analysis   102

Sample Lesson 2: Biology   102

Sample Lesson 3: Math, Art, English Project   103

Sample Lesson 4: Literary Arts Magazine   104

Sample Lesson 5: The Aunt Gladys Letter   105

Sample Lesson 6: History Magazine   108

Sample Lesson 7: History—Wagon Train 1848   111

Afterword   115

Appendix: Learning Log Procedures   116

Works Cited   118

Resources for Teachers   119

Author   121

List of Figures

1. *Twenty Questions Heuristic*   5
2. *Tagmemic Heuristic*   6
3. *Burke's Pentad*   7
4. *The "Biopoem" Template*   13
5. *Composing with Absolutes*   16
6. *Composing with Appositives*   17
7. *Composing with Participles*   18
8. *"Song of Myself" Imitation*   20
9. *Imitating Poetry Exercise*   23
10. *Writing Wall Response Sheet*   24
11. *Split Screen*   25
12. *SAT Graph*   27
13. *Business Letter Form*   29
14. *Split Screen 2*   42
15. *Audit #1*   51
16. *Group Interaction Sheet*   52
17. *Group Self-Evaluation Sheet*   53
18. *Portfolio Criteria Sheet*   57
19. *Sample Essay Criteria Form*   59
20. *Letter Criteria Sheet*   60
21. *Log-on Screens*   67
22. *Additional Screens*   71
23. *Sample Lesson File*   80
24. *Sample Screens of Magazine Layout*   92
25. *FileMaker Book Review*   99
26. *Learning Log Prompts*   100
27. *History Magazine Folder*   109

Acknowledgments

I would like to thank Kathy Marion for introducing me to my first word-processing program, for continuing to grow with the changing technology, and for challenging me to do the same. My gratitude also goes to Tom Williams, because he has the disarming quality of thinking what I have to say is important. Tom is a friend and a generous writing companion. I am grateful to Dr. Eugene Smith, University of Washington English Professor Emeritus, and to the instructors at the Lewis and Clark College Northwest Writing Institute for sparking my imagination. Finally, I would like to thank four Northshore School District colleagues: Dave Jones, my principal, because he believes schools can offer more than the mundane; Joan Fiset and Mary Kollar, two colleagues who have encouraged and nurtured my professional maturity; and Debbie Branstetter, instructional technology supervisor and friend, for her tireless efforts and vision.

I am also pleased to acknowledge the contributions of the following students, teachers, authors, and corporations for various elements used in this book: students Lisa Anderson for "Elegy to Mike" which appears on page 12, Micah Anderson for the Harvest title on page 92; teachers Fred Dahlem for the biology lesson on page 102, Joan Fiset for the Group Interaction Sheet on page 52, Andy Hegeman for the clip art exercise on page 32, Jessica Hohman Halliday for the "Drawing into Narrative" exercise on page 30, Linda Clifton for the "Delving into a Difficult Text" activity on page 41, Kathy Marion for the poem on page 42, and Holly Runyon for the math analysis on page 102 and the Math/Art/English project on page 103; authors Paul Connolly for his "Habits of Mind" descriptions on page 55 and William Wresch for the "Tagmemic Heuristic" which appears on page 6; Aldus, Apple Computers, Claris, Microsoft corporations for the various screen shots. Excerpt from *Twenty Questions for the Writer: A Rhetoric with Readings*, Second Edition by Jacqueline Berke, copyright © 1976 by Harcourt Brace & Company, reprinted by permission of the publisher.

For the "Aunt Gladys" exercise appearing in Chapter 4, permission has been given by the *Journal of Chemical Education*, which holds the copyright; the original author, Mark Ritter; and Gordon Bonnet, who wrote the biology questions I've used. Thank you, as well, is due to the Lake Washington Science Department for their assistance in rounding up all the sources that made this exercise a part of the book. The original article appears as "Bringing Science to the People—Aunt Gladys Letter," by M. Ritter, in the *Journal of Chemical Education*, 25, 1988, page 1055.

Preface

There are courses and texts about computer programs and courses and texts designed for a particular discipline, but few courses or texts, if any, show teachers how to marry both. This book attempts to bridge this gap, helping teachers use computers in a seamless way so that what and how students learn is the focus. In addition, this book is designed as a practical and progressive guide, showing how technology can be infused into the curriculum without abandoning reading, writing, thinking, listening, and speaking. Even though parts of chapter 1 and all of chapters 2 and 3 require more effort on the reader's part, because that is when I become an advocate for the local area network, what remains paramount is my firm belief that the English/language arts curriculum should be developed by committed teachers, not hardware and software representatives.

The text is divided as follows: The introduction provides the philosophical framework and rationale for an application-based computer curriculum to teach writing and thinking. In chapter 1, I present sample computer writing and thinking lessons that range from the simple to the sophisticated. Chapter 2 explains how to set up and manage a local area network, a powerful learning environment. Chapter 3 talks briefly about how to extend the uses of technology and invites the reader to imagine additional ways in which computers might extend what is already being practiced. The final chapter includes some sample lessons for teachers and administrators interested in writing across the disciplines, one of the richest uses of computer networks.

Introduction

When teachers think about incorporating computers into the curriculum, anyone within earshot can hear the resultant moans and sighs. And with good reason. Most teachers receive little help when computer labs or local area networks are installed. The more enlightened school districts include teachers in the planning process, but for the most part, the majority of a school's faculty is not involved until they are directed to find ways to use these wonderful machines. So where do teachers find the resources that will help them learn how to use computers effectively in an English/language arts class? What does the individual teacher do after the initial generic computer in-service? How does a teacher find time to include computers in an already jammed curriculum? Obviously, something must go, and in most cases, it is a teacher's patience.

This book is designed to serve English/language arts teachers, showing them ways they can incorporate computers into the already crowded curriculum. A brief philosophical explanation is provided, but it is not necessary for teachers to adopt my views. This text is predicated on the assumption that using computer applications to teach what teachers feel is important to their community is more important than buying into commercial curricular programs that require schools and teachers to modify or compromise what they value.

A Philosophical Stance

A few years ago, I made up my mind to behave as I imagined my heroes did when they taught. I simply decided to be my version of Donald Murray, Peter Elbow, James Moffett, and Louise Rosenblatt. I explained to my students that we were a community of thinkers. I told them we would make meaning in our talk, our writing, and our reading. They seemed puzzled, and that was a good start. "Our job is to wallow in chaos, get comfortable with confusion," I said. I explained that my job was to show them how to cope by giving them strategies that would help them discover and create meaning. Eventually, we would leave chaos behind and walk with understanding. Because I believed in the mind's homeostatic tendencies, its need to make meaning, all my students needed to do was to have faith that their minds would work if they embraced confusion instead of running away from it.

For the past six years, I have started the school year similarly, inviting students to become members of a thinking community, but in 1982 something happened that rocked me. I found myself in the same position as my students when the principal at St. Joseph's School announced that we had a new Apple IIe lab and that teachers would be expected to use it if they wanted to remain on staff the following year. Such a mandate might sound horrible, but for me, because I had read about word processing and had thought about how real revision would now be possible, it was also a challenge. I began by learning how to use AppleWorks, my first application.

Imagine for a moment . . . thirty students shuffle into class and sit behind their computers. Students boot up the word-processing software and open their electronic journals. After a ten-minute freewrite, three students exchange entries through the networked system and talk to each other about what they have written. After saving their comments, students open the essays they discussed in writing groups. Revision begins. Students focus on rhetorical elements saved to their stations or to the lesson folders on the network. Forty minutes into the class, each student retrieves a menu and reads the homework assignment. No one is working on the same assignment because the teacher has individualized the work, "meeting the needs of each student." Just before the bell rings, students print out the homework assignment, including the code for the online homework hotline they will access later on their home computers. That evening, teachers and students from all over the region scan the homework hotline, responding, probing, and questioning individuals who have joined this electronic learning community.

Obviously, we are not yet near this futuristic scenario. Currently, computers are toys, electronic games. Unless English teachers actively search out the possibilities for computers and get involved in the decisions that are being made, computers might as well come with slots where students can deposit quarters. Hearing coins plunk into the computer would put into perspective the existing state of computers in education. But we can change the "gimmick" appeal once we begin treating computers as important tools for thinking, problem-solving, remediation, and communication. Until we do, however, the computer is no better than an electronic crayon in the hands of a child.

Something cannot emerge from nothing. Writing about our thoughts or experiences, telling our stories, helps us understand them and act upon them. The computer does not provide the "something," but it does help in the exploring, drafting, developing, editing, and polishing of our ideas. Using computers intelligently makes the creation of a thinking and learning community possible.

The Rationale for an Application-Based Computer Curriculum

The focus of an application-based computer curriculum is to solve problems posed by students and teachers. The most prevalent application is word processing. Other applications include databases, spreadsheets, desktop publishing, and drawing programs. All of these can be integrated to help students create and present meaning. There are, of course, hundreds of computer applications and individual users have their favorites, but what is important is that they are used for doing meaningful work. All of the lessons in this book are designed to show you how a computer, like a pencil, is a useful tool and how it can help us get beyond the gimmick appeal and get on with expressing what is in our minds.

Of course, computer programs are more complicated than pencils. And some initial time must be invested to learn various programs; that needs to be made clear. Incorporating any technology, whether it is a VCR or an overhead projector, into your curriculum requires planning. But I am positive that the return on your investment will be worth the effort. Using computer applications to help you think—to draw, compile, calculate, and compose—can re-create what you currently do.

A few examples should clarify my meaning. My students meet in our school's networked computer lab once a week to draft what I call the polished piece. The polished piece is writing that students develop over ten weeks. I don't care about the form or the subject; I care only that students have an opportunity to work on a piece of their choice over time. Eventually their stories, poems, articles, and, yes, novels are submitted for publication. I have collected a list of contests for students, introduced them to the *Young Writer's Market Guide*, and, of course, included our literary arts magazine as a potential market. The other four days of the week are spent on the more traditional curriculum familiar to English/language arts teachers: reading and discussing literature, writing in learning logs (see Appendix for a discussion of learning logs), rehearsing and drafting responses to literature, meeting in writing groups, and viewing films.

As my students grow more comfortable with computers, I show them how to cut-and-paste text, find and replace words and phrases, work with several versions of the same file, and use the spell checker. I also demonstrate how to access lesson files I have developed and placed in a shared folder on the network. Generally, this kind of instruction is individual and based on the students' need to know. I walk around the lab while students are writing their polished pieces and consult with them, reading over their shoulders, answering questions specific to a particular writing task, and encouraging these young writers to write on.

I also encourage my students to talk and to move around. The tone in the computer lab is friendly but business-like. Sometimes I will ask a student if I can have a printout to share with the rest of the class. On those occasions, I make an overhead transparency and then we celebrate an image, a fine sentence, or some element of writing I would like others to attempt. These mini-lessons last about ten minutes. You wouldn't believe how much goodwill this produces. I also display student work on the PC viewer. As a class we can talk about organization, and I can cut-and-paste the text immediately, showing the class the results of their suggestions. Even when the work is in progress, students see their peers as published writers, those whose work is usually preserved only in dusty anthologies. It is amazing how much is accomplished in such a ten-minute show-and-tell presentation.

As the year progresses, so too does our sophistication in using computer applications in the lab. For example, sometimes we meet in the lab for an extra day to respond to a prompt or quotation I saved in a shared folder. Students log-on, open the "read only" file (a file to which the students may not make changes), and then are given ten minutes to write a response. Subsequently, the students move over to another computer two or three seats away where they read the first timed writing and then write a response to it. Students repeat this pattern three or four times, writing responses to the previous timed writings before they return to their original terminals and print out the accumulated responses. Students take the printouts home and read them over. The next day, we launch into a class discussion. Sometimes, we go directly to writing groups, where students talk about the responses. And sometimes, we conduct a read-around so the entire class can hear what others have said.

We use many more strategies, and this book includes them as well. I hope you are intrigued. More important, I hope you are beginning to see how incorporating computers into the curriculum can enrich both teachers and students.

1 Computers in the Classroom

Teachers need to know that working with computers is both rewarding and demanding. The rewards are recognizable; you will be able to design lessons that focus on the process of articulating thought, discovering that working with computers invites sincere conversations between you and your students. There are also demands associated with using computers in the classroom, but they are manageable because they tend to be procedural. For example: what happens when a student logs-on and gets an error message or the printer runs out of paper? One of the demands that may cause teachers quite a bit of anxiety is imagining how to design meaningful lessons with this technology. This, of course, may require redefining the teacher's role, one of the most stressful aspects of any classroom endeavor.

If you are a new user, then keep in mind that we all tend to resist the unfamiliar. Teachers will not value the learning students might do with a computer until they use one in their professional lives. It is difficult, and perhaps impossible, to imagine how to incorporate computers into the existing curriculum without first experiencing the frustration and pleasure every learner undergoes.

Thinking about a computer as a tool to make something is a start, but I would like to suggest an even more philosophical approach. A computer **is** a tool. I am not suggesting, however, that it is similar to a hammer, drill press, or even a microwave oven. The effectiveness of any tool is limited by its function and by the imagination and skill of the user. English teachers do not have to become computer experts; our expertise is language, the tool we use to extend thought. I suppose that's why I don't mind thinking of myself as a computer apprentice.

I care that, as a tool, the computer frees me and my students from the barriers extant in an older technology such as the pen. We can use computers to join and extend conversations important to us. We can focus on meaning over time because this new tool suggests some of the ephemeral qualities found in oral dialogue. Text generated on a computer screen can be erased, edited, massaged. It is fluid, like spoken language. I realize I am taking a generous stance, but my philosophical position as a teacher is inclusive rather than exclusive. It should be obvious by now that I am not interested in only the utilitarian uses of language. Of course, I am not much interested in prefabricated housing developments either. I am vitally curious about new designs, how one person manipulates language and expresses thought.

Motivating Students to Write

When a student writes using a computer, ideas flow from the student's mind to the keyboard to the screen. The words dance across the monitor as the student writes, the cursor blinking incessantly, urging the student to continue. Because words are so easily moved and removed from the screen, the student is not as stubborn about editing his or her writing. Changing something simply is not as laborious as it used to be. If the student is willing to experiment with the text, testing the writer's intent against the reader's understanding, then the relationship between reader and writer, or audience and performer, can be forged. A student who understands, even vaguely, such a relationship will be a more purposeful and considerate writer.

Additionally, the computer allows me to act less like a teacher and more like a consultant. My students feel free to ask me questions about the development or arrangement of text because changing and rearranging their work is not traumatic. Thus, I find myself moving around the computer lab consulting with students who have specific questions of this nature.

Computers have made the physical act of writing less messy. With computers, students do not have scratched out paragraphs or words smeared across the paper. Now, with a few keystrokes, students can effortlessly arrange or rearrange text. Because the physical act of writing is easier, students are willing to spend more time on their writing. Any tool that can be used to lessen the strain of copying words onto paper will eventually motivate students to work on their writing.

In the past, motivating students to grapple with written expression as a way of discovering meaning was difficult. My students now relish the time they spend working with computers, even if they do have to work on a writing assignment. No longer do I coax or cajole my students into developing an idea. Their only complaint now is that they do not get to spend enough time writing and thinking with the computer. And because I believe that time spent practicing anything is beneficial, I can expect to see much more improvement in my students' work.

Of course, I cannot relinquish my responsibilities. I still have usage and punctuation skills to teach. I still have to develop a trusting environment for my students. I still have to monitor their progress, providing the necessary guidance or intervention: I still have to help my students grow. The computer cannot transform students into an Atwood or an Einstein. This teaching method is a challenge and, although I am excited, I am also cautious.

A Cautionary Word to Teachers

As an English teacher who has thirty computers in a networked configuration available to me and my students (a lab that offers everything from word-processing to desktop-publishing software), every year I am both enthusiastic and reticent. At the beginning of a new year, I have that same feeling I had when sentence combining was touted as the cure for my students' syntactic idiosyncracies. I learned a hard lesson: sentence combining was one kind of editing tool, but I still had to teach my students prewriting, arrangement, form, voice, audience, purpose, punctuation, and any element of composing required to communicate. I still had to teach writing, critical thinking, listening, speaking, and reading. Computers can be useful, but they are not a panacea.

A computer is an information processor, dependent on the user's ability to put information into it and then transform that information in a meaningful way. A computer is not simply an output device; it is not a glorified typewriter. Even so, one real roadblock for most users is typing. What good is word-processing software if students cannot type? The computer supposedly makes writing easier because it allows students to make textual changes faster than they can physically cut and paste text or erase and rewrite. Even though the computer can help students think about information in new ways through charts, graphics, and scanned images, it cannot create. Meaning is still the domain of the human mind.

Problems for Students

Before teachers get too excited about this wonderful tool, they should not overlook the basic knowledge and skill required of every computer user. Our goal is defeated if our students spend twenty minutes pecking out a paragraph on the computer. Even my slowest student can write a paragraph by hand in less than twenty minutes. Luckily, "typing tutor" software is abundant and inexpensive, so learning how to keyboard is one of the simplest hurdles to overcome. If students spend less time editing and writing a clean final draft, they have more thinking time. The ability to use computers as tools can give students a psychological edge as well. Computers can make this one aspect of composing less time-consuming and, therefore, less painful. However, without basic typing skills, say twenty words a minute, we might confound our students. Without realizing it, we might be telling these students they cannot think with either a pencil or a computer.

Computers should not frighten us. They are tools for writing and thinking, but the writing and thinking processes still emanate from the human mind. The computer allows us to edit, work on style, separate ourselves from our words, rearrange text, and experiment with form—all this with relative ease. Keep in mind that our subject knowledge, our ability to assess student progress, and our willingness to challenge students constitute every teacher's primary role. Including computers as part of the curriculum does not change the fact that teachers must continue to act as compassionate and knowledgeable guides.

Electronic Read-Arounds and Other Computer-Writing Strategies

Technology has given writing teachers and their students a powerful writing tool and ally: the computer. As a tool, the computer has increased the fluency of my reluctant writers. And as an ally, the computer has led ordinarily apathetic students to enjoy their work in the lab. Teaching with a computer has made discovering the intricacies of writing and thinking a more efficient and rewarding experience for me and my students.

Let me explain how my students apply writing with a computer to the process-oriented model of composition. After a writing assignment is given or a deadline is set for a student-initiated piece, we go to the lab to start discovering and drafting. Priming the pump, prewriting, is important, so I allow students one class period to either cluster (discovering how words, concepts, and impressions are related) in their learning logs or freewrite directly on the computer. Some of my students prefer clustering on paper, searching for an emerging point of view or additional details before they begin writing. Many, however, have grown used to what Stephen Marcus (1990) calls "invisible writing" (p. 9): turning the contrast of the monitor down and writing nonstop, usually in fits and bursts. Students then turn up the contrast to see what they have written. The computer's editing flexibility really works against productive freewriting. Invisible writing sidesteps this trap. This technique seems more productive for pickier students, those who are tempted to go back and make changes before discovering what they have to say.

(X = any subject)

1. What does X mean?
2. How can X be described?
3. What are the parts of X?
4. How is X made or done?
5. How should X be made or done?
6. What is the essential function of X?
7. What are the causes of X?
8. What are the consequences of X?
9. What are the types of X?
10. How does X compare to Y?
11. What is the present status of X?
12. How can X be interpreted?
13. What are the facts about X?
14. How did X happen?
15. What kind of person/thing is X?
16. What is your personal response to X?
17. What is your memory of X?
18. What is the value of X?
19. How can X be summarized?
20. What case can be made for or against X?

Figure 1. Twenty Questions Heuristic, from J. Berke, *Twenty Questions for the Writer*.

After all the students have written something they can commit time to, we begin developing a topic. There are several good software programs that help students develop and arrange ideas. One of the best is Writer's Helper, a program developed by William Wresch. It is helpful to acquire software that asks the kinds of questions found in Burke's pentad (see Figure 3) or Wresch's Tagmemic Heuristic (see Figure 2) and that can run rudimentary style checking. However, I am opposed to buying software that promises too much. Writer's Helper, if used judiciously, if used as Wresch recommends, can enhance what we do in writing groups and student/teacher conferences. Like most schools, however, mine could not afford a site license for additional software

1. What would be a good brief description of . . .

2. What is the dominant characteristic of . . .

3. How would you best describe the importance of . . .

4. What makes people most attracted to . . .

5. What is least attractive about . . .

6. What has changed about the importance of . . .

7. Are people more or less attracted to . . .

8. In the future what might people become most attracted to about . . .

9. What used to be least attractive to people about . . .

10. Why has there been this change in the attractiveness of . . .

11. How could you compare your subject's appearance to similar . . .

12. In what ways may your subject's appearance be worse than other . . .

13. How is your subject more important than other . . .

14. How is your subject less important than similar . . .

15. What about your subject is better than similar . . .

16. What about your subject is worse than . . .

Figure 2. Tagmemic Heuristic, from W. Wresch, *Writer's Helpful Handbook.*

such as Writer's Helper, so I have learned to make better use of our word-processing and networking software by creating what I call lesson files.

Developing a heuristic lesson file is easy. Simply enter the information you want into the file and either save it in a shared folder over the network (a folder to which all students have access) or onto student storage disks. Make sure you provide one or two spaces between each prompt so students can easily insert their responses.

After students complete the first draft of a writing assignment, they can use the lesson files shown in Figures 1–3 to explore their initial drafts. At the top of each heuristic file, I have typed the following instructions:

> The following questions are meant to help you discover what you might want to say. To make the heuristic work for you, try to answer every prompt that applies to your topic as completely as you can. Do not worry about censoring your ideas—just let everything out that comes to mind.

1. What happened? (Action)

2. Who/what did it? (Agent)

3. Where did it happen or what is the background? (Scene)

4. How did the agent do it? (Means)

5. Why or why not? (Purpose)

Figure 3. Burke's Pentad.

Figure 1 is the Twenty Questions Heuristic. Students use the questions to analyze their work, substituting their chosen subject for the X in each question. Figure 2 illustrates the Tagmemic Heuristic. Here, students use these questions to find out more about their subject, expanding the focus of their work. Figure 3 is a representation of Burke's famous pentad. Students can use this pentad to ask questions about their writing. (Teachers will find an excellent discussion of Burke's pentad in William Irmsher's 1981 book, *The Holt Guide to English*, 3rd edition.)

If students have difficulty finding something more to say in their drafts, I suggest retrieving one of these lesson files. Even after students have dedicated some time to a piece of writing, say between two and four sessions in the computer lab, I still urge them to use one of these lesson files to examine their texts. Students should read through the file and answer any questions they think were not adequately developed. Used this way, a lesson file can be a powerful aid for the expansion of ideas.

Electronic Read-Arounds

Eventually, students are ready for feedback. Normally, we print hard copies of our work and meet in writing groups the next day in class. Lately, however, we have been doing what I call electronic read-arounds. Here is how it works. Students retrieve their files and then depress the CAPS LOCK key or change to a different font. Then, everyone moves over two or three chairs to a different computer. Readers follow the same procedure we use in class: They read the drafts all the way through. Readers then read the text again, this time responding to the content, inserting their comments right on the screen. Because the CAPS LOCK key is engaged or the font is *different*, the reader's comments *stand out* from the writer's text. We shift seats about every ten minutes or so. A writer can receive as many as four honest and detailed responses in a normal class period.

Near the end of the period, students return to their original computers. The writers now have several choices. They can save the files with the comments littering their drafts, rename the files and save them so the original file remains unblemished, or ignore the comments and shut down the computer. Rarely do students ignore their peers' comments. Most of my students rename and save the files replete with comments. The benefits are obvious. Besides being fun, this activity allows students to read pieces from classmates not in their own writing groups. When they retrieve the files later, writers get feedback that points to where or how they might revise. In addition, the integrity of the original file can be retained, provided it was renamed. I firmly believe in avoiding premature evaluation. Electronic read-arounds accomplish this, because students are focused on the development of their writing.

A natural extension of the above activity is what Jamieson McKenzie (1984) calls "accordion writing." Jamieson talks about encouraging students to use the computer to expand and compress text. Students arrange blocks of writing that seem related and then insert additional thoughts afterward. Students delete ideas or comments made during the ensuing electronic read-around that are not valuable and develop those that are more promising. Of course, the writer will have to decide which reader's comments should be ignored and which should be expanded.

Ways to Respond in Writing Groups

To make student writing groups more effective, to assist listeners so they can actively help each other, I model ways students can respond. Each strategy demands specific feedback writers may find useful. Students need to know that using any of these techniques may seem awkward at first, but that is okay; doing something new always feels odd.

All of the strategies here can be used in a networked or stand-alone computer lab. To begin, ask students to open the writing they are currently working on and then instruct them to open the "Helping Writers" file. This lesson file informs students how they are going to "hear" the writing in progress. After everyone has read the "Helping Writers" file, students close this file, leaving their own writing displayed on the screen. Then they move over three chairs and read another student's work twice. After the second reading, they respond to this writing at the end of the student's draft.

For example, if Pointing is the method students are to use, it will be in the shared folder. The first reader opens the shared folder and follows the directions. He or she enters a list of all the memorable words or images in the draft he or she has read at the end of the writer's file. Ask "listeners" (readers) to tap the return key three or four times after they have finished their lists. Then, ask the students to move over three more chairs, repeating the cycle three or four times. This is the same technique described in "Electronic Read-Arounds" except that, in this case, the prompt (e.g., Pointing) informs students how they should respond to each other's drafts. By the end of the period, writers should have three or four responses they can print out and examine later as they continue to develop their poems, stories, or essays.

Even though students enjoy this kind of electronic writing group, I use it sparingly. I believe writers and listeners need to face each other and to hear what each other has to say, so most writing-group sessions are held in my classroom, not in the networked computer lab. It is easy to get caught up in the technology of computer-assisted writing, so be careful to question when and how it is used.

What follows are the listening strategies I model and my students use when they meet in writing groups:

Pointing (echoing back): What words, phrases, or images stand out? Point to them by entering the words as a kind of list; it is all right if several responders point to the same things. This strategy is used when a writer wants confirmation that something in the writing has had an effect, but he or she is not ready for more specific feedback. Listeners point to specifics without discussion. This is a good starting point for other kinds of feedback.

Active Listening (say back): Listeners say, in their own words, what they hear the writer saying—to make room for the writer to say more. Generally, Active Listening is posed as a kind of question: "So are you saying that...?" In Active Listening, readers try to get writers to say more about their pieces; it invites writers to explore their subjects, to grope further for something new, without referring to what has been done before as if the work were a finished piece of writing, thinking, or experiencing. The object is not for listeners to "get it right," but to help writers discover their ideas.

Center of Gravity: Listeners say what they hear as the heart of a piece—its focus: "Your main idea seems to be..." Peter Elbow made this strategy famous. This is a more focused, analytic kind of listening. Center of Gravity helps the writer identify the main point, assertion, or thesis. With early drafts, this strategy helps a writer find the thesis; with later drafts, it confirms the focus.

Believing and Doubting: Again this strategy comes from Elbow, and the idea is to listen two ways. The listener first suspends disbelief in the author's assertions and supports the ideas; then, the listener takes the opposite approach and, without argument, lists some doubts about these same ideas. The listener questions the writing in order to improve it. There are several points in the writing process when employing Believing and Doubting can be effective:

- when the writing is finished, but it feels unsatisfying to the reader or the writer or both.

- when the claims, logic, or conception of a piece feel problematic or seem to beg some confirmation.

- when a writer feels confident and wants to elaborate more.

When using this strategy, both writer and listener must be sensitive to one another's feelings.

Lurkings: What do listeners almost hear? What is circling around the edges? Where does the piece want to go? What do listeners want to hear more about? Lurkings are posed as probative, exploratory kinds of questions. Lurkings help the writer push a piece of writing to uncover possibilities. Listeners are inviting new thinking and discovery. For example, a reader might ask: "Why don't you say more about X?"

Suggestions: "If I were writing this I would . . . because I . . ." This strategy should be used late in the process of writing and only if the writer finds it easy to say "no." Listeners must explain why they would make the suggested changes.

Collaborative Writing

Collaborative writing is another technique I have brought to the computer lab. Because I believe in talking through an idea, I set up times in the year when students can collaborate on an essay. Any teacher who has asked students to write a collaborative piece knows the inherent pitfalls. Group writing requires more talking. It is a noisy business. One good way to keep students on task is to have the group meet in front of a computer where one student has retrieved the Tagmemic Heuristic (Figure 2) file. Three members of the group stand around the monitor applying the questions to their topic, while the fourth member enters their responses. Having the group respond to the heuristic not only keeps students on task but also helps them consider directions they might otherwise overlook. When we write a collaborative piece, I let partners decide how to divide up the computer time. Some groups take turns at the keyboard. Others let the fastest typist do all the keyboarding. It does not really matter, because the real work begins when the students start revising.

Once the groups have worked out their directions, development time is needed. At this point, I have students save the group-generated text onto their own storage disks or in a shared folder on the network. Each member of the group is now expected to develop one paragraph for the essay. After members of the group have finished their contributions, the separate files are merged and saved as one file. Introductions and conclusions are written by the group.

Collaborative writing naturally results in poor transitions and other inconsistencies, so extra time for revising and editing is required. At this point in the project, several paths are possible. The groups can print their drafts and meet in writing groups, or the class can conduct an electronic read-around. It is better to use both strategies, once during the development stage and once afterwards. I prefer doing a group electronic read-around of the merged file first. Students follow the same procedure described earlier. Groups rotate, reading and commenting on the collaborative piece. Students know the drafts are incomplete, so they provide helpful comments about transitions and development. Time is then given for group revision and editing before publication.

Although time-consuming, collaborative writing is one valuable way to avoid mental meltdown. It seems to me a natural solution. I am always amazed at how cooperative and insightful students can be when they get excited about an idea. I have overheard groups justifying and developing ideas, disputing the placement of paragraphs, and questioning development. I never get tired of watching students talk about which paragraph should be placed where or whether this word is better than that word. It is rewarding to see students working together on something they think is important.

More about Lesson Files and Shared Folders

While you read through this book, bear in mind that it reflects what I and my colleagues think is important. We are not tied to lessons created by a commercial developer, because our lab is application based. We use general word-processing programs to create our own lessons. This is a significant point. The curriculum described in this book was developed by knowledgeable teachers for real students, not by commercial developers for imaginary students.

As explained in the previous chapter, a lesson file is a good way to begin creating a flexible curriculum. An entire folder filled with writing models can be created for student use. If you do not have a networked lab, you can copy a disk filled with samples of writing that students can read and then imitate later. In a stand-alone configuration, you might label disks Writing Models. In addition to some professional works, I suggest most of the models include exemplary student work.

In our networked lab, when students open the Models folder, they see a list of files that are titles of poems, stories, and essays. Much like flipping through an anthology, students scroll through the files, opening those that seem interesting. For example, the following poem was written by Lisa Anderson, a former English 11 student. It was modeled after Theodore Roethke's "Elegy for Jane." If a student opened Lisa's file in the Models folder, this is what he or she would see:

Elegy for Mike

I remember the eyes, blue
  and clear as water,
And his face, his gentle
  attentive look;
And how, once started into a smile,
  the soft innocence radiated from
  him.
And he balanced in the thought
  of his friends.
An eagle, flying, wings into the
  wind.
His leadership guiding friends
  and family.
The shade rested with him;
The trees, their swaying,
  turned to dancing.
And the animals played in the
  flowing rivers in the forest.

When he was sad, he cast
  himself down into such a troubling
  depth,
Even a friend could not find him:
Thinking his mind openly;
Sparking the deepest thoughts.
My Eagle, you are not here,
Loving like a brother, keeping a
  strict watch.
The clouds of the bluest skies
  cannot console me,
Nor the light, streaming from the
  brightest sun.

If only I could nudge you from
   this sleep,
My lost friend, my only
   brother.
Over this damp grave I speak the
   words of my love.
I with no peaceful soul,
   Neither awake nor asleep.

Take a moment to read Roethke's poem after enjoying Lisa's. You can find the original poem on page 701 of the *Adventures in American Literature* anthology. You might try writing your own version, following the same patterns and images.

Shared folders can be set up with any networking software. Because the lesson files are created with a word-processing program and saved in a shared folder, the files do not take up much hard disk

---

A *Biopoem* follows this pattern:

Line 1. First name

Line 2. Four traits that describe the character

Line 3. Relative ("brother," "sister," "daughter," etc.) of_____

Line 4. Lover of_____ (list three things or people)

Line 5. Who feels_____ (three items)

Line 6. Who needs_____ (three items)

Line 7. Who fears_____ (three items)

Line 8. Who gives_____ (three items)

Line 9. Who would like to see_____ (three items)

Line 10. Resident of_____

Line 11. Last name

The above pattern is meant to help you get started; it is not a strict format. Play around with the eleven starters. You might also want to rearrange some of the lines using the cut-and-paste features of the computer. To add some semblance of balance, however, I would like you to leave lines one and eleven in their original positions.

When you finish drafting, be sure to delete the instructions and the line numbers that begin each starter; then title your biopoem. As always, save your biopoem, using your name and today's date, in the appropriate folder or on your own disk.

Figure 4. The ''Biopoem'' Template.

storage and can be easily adapted by the teacher and accessed by students.

For example, when studying a novel, you might ask students to write a biopoem about an important character as a way to describe that character and step into the literature. A biopoem helps a student see how a character's actions and words come together. In our networked lab, students log-on as usual; then they open the Monroe folder, which contains all of my classes and an additional folder called Assignments. The Assignments folder, like the Models folder, lets students open and read files and work with them, but they cannot save any alterations made to the original file. After working with a shared file, my students rename it and either save the file to their own disks or to our class folder on the network.

So, if I want to assign a specific kind of response to a piece of literature, I direct my students to the Assignments folder. If a student opens the file named "Biopoem," the template in Figure 4 appears.

Here is a sample lesson file my seniors responded to from the Assignments folder. It comes from Annie Dillard's (1986) essay "Living Like Weasels." We read the essay in class and then moved to the networked computer lab where students were instructed to open the shared file "Weasels." My students know that after logging-on, they are to open the Assignments folder and then retrieve the desired file, following its instructions. Because it is a shared folder, the networking software always warns students that they will receive a "read only" file; they do not have the access privileges to save changes to this particular file. The networking software allows students to read the file, but when they need to save their own work, they must rename the file and save it elsewhere. Remember, any networking software does not allow students to save over files that are shared.

This is what my students saw when they opened the "Weasels" file:

> Now that you have read "Living Like Weasels," merged it with "Snake," and read your mergings to your core group, I would like you to pay particular attention to the following excerpt from Dillard's essay. Read what she says and then respond to it. You have six minutes.
>
> > I would like to live as I should, as the weasel lives as he should. And I suspect that for me the way is like the weasel's: open to time and death painlessly, noticing everything, remembering nothing, choosing the given with a fierce and pointed will. I missed my chance. (pp. 1449–53)

As explained in "Electronic Read-Arounds and Other Computer Writing Strategies," students read the prompt and then responded to it. Then I directed individuals to move over three computer stations. Their task was to read the response and expand or question it, extending the conversation originally established. After about ten to twelve minutes, students moved again, responding to both entries. I generally tried to encourage three or four such exchanges before asking students to return to their original stations. Near the end of the class, the students saved their files, using their names and the date for the filenames. Then they printed their files. This procedure is a kind of electronic dialectical notebook.

The Quaker Read-Around

A fun and useful way to follow up an electronic dialectical notebook activity is to ask students to read over their printouts at home and then bring them to class the following day. At the beginning of the class, ask students to mark ideas, whether their own or someone else's, that seem important to them. Tell them they are now going to reconstruct the original text and their thoughts concerning it in a *Quaker Read-Around.*

As you are probably aware, Quakers do not have ministers. They hold services where they gather to listen to their consciences, sitting quietly and listening. At some point, when the moment is right, one member of the congregation says what is on his or her mind. After a moment of reflection, another member says something, generally a response to what was previously stated.

Students can imitate a Quaker service by waiting, listening, and responding to each other, using the marked sections from their printouts. I like to turn down the lights in my room to help create a serious mood. And then we begin. It's amazing how this technique can illuminate a text, making it accessible in a way a teacher-led discussion cannot.

The Sentence Composing Lesson Folder

I also use shared lesson files to help students play with sentence style. I have created a separate folder called Sentence Style. The idea, like most in this book, is simple. I want my students to experience and attend to models that help them gain control of their writing and thinking. Until I discovered Don Killgallon's sentence composing texts, I was not satisfied with how I taught style. My English department purchased class sets of *Sentence Composing 10, Sentence Composing 11,*

Composing with Absolutes

An absolute phrase is a modifier that grammatically resembles a complete sentence. Every absolute phrase includes a subject and a partial verb, which is why it resembles a complete sentence. However, because the verb is not complete, absolutes are considered phrases and not clauses. Missing in every absolute phrase is an auxiliary verb—almost always a form of the verb *to be* (*is, are, was,* or *were*). Another distinguishing characteristic of a majority of absolute phrases is the kind of word they usually begin with, such as *This, her, their,* or *its.*

The following samples should give you an idea how absolute phrases work. The absolute phrase is **highlighted.** Note how the absolute phrase is always separated from the rest of the sentence by a comma or commas.

His squinting eyes surveying the crowd, the Mayor smiled and nodded at their approval.

The room, **its barren walls fading into oblivion**, seemed vacant even though twenty people were crowded inside.

Directions

Read the following sentences and:

- make the absolute phrase bold, including the punctuation mark(s).

- write your own sentence, imitating the model.

After you complete five sentences, delete the above definition and directions. Do not delete the title of this lesson. At the top left, type your name, date, and period.

1. High on the bluff, his hands thrust into his pockets, Slim scanned the desert valley below in search of life.

2. John walked with a strut, his cowboy boots echoing throughout the saloon.

3. Outside, her parasol gingerly held in her small hands, Sheila scanned the remote Montana town as she stepped from the stagecoach.

4. Elmer sat in a heap outside the saloon, his once majestic posture ruined from riding broncos.

5. Its streets muddy after the spring rain, Bozeman smelled rich with manure and promise.

Figure 5. Composing with Absolutes.

and *Sentence Composing 12.* After working through Killgallon's models, I realized they could prove useful in our networked computer lab. Killgallon's books are more complete than what I present in this book, so I encourage you to examine his series. Even so, I have taken one of his suggestions and incorporated it into a shared lesson file.

After students log-on, they go to the Sentence Style folder. In it they have three choices: Composing with Absolutes, Composing with

---

Composing with Appositives

An appositive is a word or group of words that identifies (renames) an adjacent word or group of words. An appositive phrase is the appositive word plus any of its modifiers. Most commonly, appositives are nouns that rename other nouns. The examples below should clarify the above definition. The appositive phrase is in bold. Notice how the appositive phrase is punctuated.

Dad, **a quiet man,** spent much of his time working hard to keep the family together during the Depression.

The boy looked at them, **big red insects.**

Directions

Read the following sentences and:

■ make the appositive phrase bold, including the punctuation mark(s).

■ write your own sentence, imitating the model.

After you complete five sentences, delete the above definition and directions. Do not delete the title of this lesson. At the top left, type your name, date, and period.

1. A tall lanky man, Slim scanned the desert valley below in search of life.

2. John, an arrogant gunslinger, walked with a strut, his cowboy boots echoing throughout the saloon.

3. Outside, her parasol gingerly held in her small hands, Sheila, a demure and pretty widow, scanned the remote Montana town.

4. Elmer sat in a heap outside the saloon, a broken-down building that used to be a gathering place for cowboys.

5. Bozeman, a wide-open cattle town, smelled rich with manure and promise.

Figure 6. Composing with Appositives.

Appositives, and Composing with Participles. Figure 5 shows the Composing with Absolutes file.

You can design your own Sentence Style lesson files. Decide for yourself, based on your students' needs and motivation, how you would design the lessons. I broke up the sentences in groups of five and asked my students to do five imitations a week on their own time. Even though I only provide one set of five sentences as examples here, I included six sets of five sentences on our network. Students visited the computer lab and completed the lessons, and we spent a few minutes once a week writing a few examples on the chalkboard in the classroom, noting especially fine imitations. Whenever I spied an absolute in their writing or in a text we were reading, I noted it so my students would see that style was more than luck.

Composing with Participles

A participle phrase is a modifier of a noun or pronoun. The first word in the participle phrase is usually the participle itself. There are two types of participles. Those called present participles end in -*ing*. Those ending in either -*ed* or -*en* are called past participles. The examples below should clarify the above definition. The participle phrase is in bold. Notice how the participle phrase is punctuated.

Standing there in the middle of the crowd, the Mayor smiled and nodded at their approval.

The room, **illuminated by a single bulb,** seemed barren even though twenty people were crowded inside.

Directions

Read the following sentences and:

- make the participle phrase bold, including the punctuation mark(s).

- write your own sentence, imitating the model.

After you complete five sentences, delete the above definition and directions. Do not delete the title of this lesson. At the top left, type your name, date, and period.

1. Scanning the desert valley below, Slim wondered if anything or anyone could live there.

2. John, walking with a strut into the saloon, suspiciously surveyed the patrons.

3. Twirling her parasol gingerly, Sheila, a demure and pretty widow, scanned the remote Montana town.

4. Sitting in a heap outside the saloon, Elmer watched the gathering cowboys.

5. Sometimes a group of them came to the saloon, filling the room with cigar smoke and the rich smell of manure.

Figure 7. Composing with Participles.

I have included the samples of appositive and participle lesson files (See Figures 6 and 7) in case you are interested in using them with your students. If you want to use them, all you need to do is enter them onto the computers you and your students use. If you are using a networked lab, see your networking handbook to make these lesson files shared files. If you are using a stand-alone computer lab, or if you have only a few computers in your room, you will need to create separate files on disks. In a stand-alone configuration, lesson files can become a nightmare because students can save over the originals unless these files are originally saved as templates. Therefore, you need to make sure students are well-versed in renaming files, or you need to train a few reliable students who can check and recopy the original files if they are changed inadvertently.

I used the same sentences for each composing model on purpose so students could concentrate on the pattern of the sentences being imitated. When practicing with models, the structure is more important than the meaning, and students recognize this. They will accept imitation as rehearsal, provided you do not spend too much time drilling them on points of applied grammar and punctuation. Students already think that knowing the names of parts of speech and usage rules constitutes a mastery over language. It is important, then, to keep these kinds of lessons brief, say ten to fifteen minutes. And they should be fun as well.

Sometimes I exaggerate one of the models by embedding two or three additional phrases, expanding a sentence to over sixty words. On these occasions, I bring a PC viewer to class so that I can project what is on the computer screen for the whole class to see. I ask a student volunteer to enter his or her imitation. Then, with the class offering suggestions, we expand the imitation as in the following example. The original sentence read:

> The hunter unsheathed the knife and finished the work, slicing the throat of the enormous animal.

The student imitation read:

> The teacher uncapped the pen and finished writing, slicing the student's poem in half.

My students and I have had so much fun playing with the sentence patterns demonstrated in Killgallon's books that we have written sentences well over a hundred words long. Here is a sentence my students and I generated. I used the PC viewer to project their suggestions:

> Nibbling on her lower lip, tapping her right toe against the desk, bending over the stack of student papers, glancing nervously out the school room window, the teacher uncapped her pen and finished writing, slicing the student's poem in half, nodding slowly at her comments, watching its life bleed away, wondering if the dean would hire her back next autumn.

More about Modeling

Exercises meant to be done at the sentence level can be replicated at the paragraph (or higher) level, particularly if you have access to a PC viewer. This is a device that projects, via an overhead projector, what

---

"Song of Myself" Imitation

Walt Whitman wrote "Song of Myself" in 1855. This poem was inspired by the idea that everyone is connected, that because we have all lived and shared sights, sounds, and feelings about life, we can understand and value one another. This concept presents the challenge of exploring the past, present, and future in a personal way.

Using "Song of Myself" as a model, write a free verse poem that is a song of yourself. Try to forget your limitations and write as Whitman did, seeing yourself as a person who sees, hears, feels, and understands all of life. Imagine yourself in many different places, including places you've never been. Let your poem keep changing subjects as it goes along.

To begin, use the following starters. Add at least five specific images and details under each starter as a way to generate ideas. When you finish, delete these directions, type your name, date, and period number at the top right-hand corner, and then SAVE this file with your name, some abbreviation of the poem, and today's date. Don't forget to print what you've started.

"Song of Myself" Starters

When I am silent I hear . . .

I stand still and see . . .

I feel . . .

I understand . . .

List five injustices you are aware of from the past or present.

Make a list of attributes you possess. Don't be shy; be bold, even boastful.

Figure 8. "Song of Myself" Imitation.

is displayed on a computer screen. I use the PC viewer to teach lab procedures, but even if you don't have a networked or stand-alone computer lab, you can teach students a lot about writing with one computer and a PC viewer. For example, as part of the year-end book my juniors produce, they are expected to write several kinds of poems. One of the requirements is an imitation of Walt Whitman's "Song of Myself." I adapted Joan Hamilton's lesson from *The English Classroom in the Computer Age: Thirty Lesson Plans*, asking students to use the pattern in Figure 8 to generate their own version.

I brought a computer and a PC viewer into my class, retrieved the "Song of Myself" lesson file, and spent fifteen to twenty minutes asking my students to help me draft my "Song of Myself." I intentionally kept the lesson brief, demonstrating how to insert text, making lists, and generating as much about each prompt as possible.

At first, I simply scrolled through the lesson file and asked students to make suggestions. I told them we were brainstorming, using the prompts as guides. In just a few minutes, we generated a list of ideas for the first prompt. I scrolled to one that looked interesting, and we generated another list. (Generally, this is enough to demonstrate that what we are trying to do is freewrite.) I then scrolled back up to an idea from the first list and began adding details. Students knew that the arrangement of the above prompts was arbitrary because we started cutting and pasting the raw writing, moving the text for effect. In less than twenty minutes, we generated enough raw material for me to begin drafting an earnest version of my "Song of Myself."

It should be noted that someone always interrupts me and asks, "How did you do that?" This is a perfect time to show the class how they can arrange lines or blocks of text with the computer. As I mentioned before, the best time to teach a feature of an application is when a student needs to know it. It's important that these kinds of lessons be kept short. I try to design lessons that compel students to ask about application features such as cut-and-paste. I also make sure that what I demonstrate takes less than half the class period, because it is essential for students to begin working on *their* writing.

Two days later, I posted the following version on the writing wall:

A Song for My Students
by Rick Monroe
(with apologies to Walt Whitman)

When I am silent I hear my students'
pencils scraping across paper.
Their pages flutter under my eyelids and
I hear their clicking keyboards, like rain,
tap dancing through my sleep.
When I am quiet, at rest,
I hear the murmur of their
thoughts lulling me into dreams.

I understand they have dreams and,
like the heart of a child, their writing reminds me
that nobody is perfect, that—
    friends are more valuable than books,
    homework gets lost and
    parents sometimes press too much.

But they buoy me in their
struggle to own their souls.
They know more than money talks.
    My students dream big and
haven't sold out.
They believe in justice and love—

that the KKK cannot survive and
that another Holocaust will not occur
that we can all live in peace.
I have faith in the human heart, because
my students teach me.

When I stand still, I read their hope,
like a lighthouse beacon,
scanning the sea. I see the spark
in their eyes and hear their voices,
"Come join us; we are all the same."

If I trust them,
if I listen, and
watch them
my students will make
a way I can follow.

Normally, a lesson file as intricate as "Song of Myself" can cause a lot of frustration, but because I walked students through my own version, they were able to explore their versions more easily. Because I used the PC viewer, opened the lesson file and demonstrated the procedures they would use in our networked lab, elicited suggestions for the above prompts and worked through the lesson file with them, students were able to work productively in the lab.

After students are familiar with the computer lab procedures and computer applications, you might assign homework you have placed in a shared folder. The lesson in Figure 9 paralleled the reading we were doing in class. I did not feel we could afford taking two more days away from class discussions and writing groups, so I typed another poetry assignment and inserted it in the Monroe Assignments folder. I assigned a due date when the imitations had to be posted on the writing wall.

Our networked computer lab is open an hour before and after school and during all three lunch periods, so I feel comfortable assigning the kind of lesson described next. You will have to make provisions and adjustments depending on your situations.

In this case, when one of my students opened the "Imitating Poetry" lesson file they saw what appears in Figure 9.

I mentioned the writing wall, so I would like to talk about it here. My students publish their work in many ways, but one of them is the writing wall. I set aside a large section of a wall where students literally post their drawings and drafts. To avoid the student-to-teacher response cycle, I ask students to read what is on the writing wall. After

---

Imitating Poetry

The following poems appear in this lesson. The ones in bold have directions with them. Make sure you read these directions before you begin working with the poem of your choice.

At The Site Of Last Night's Fire

Dreams

Elegy for Mike

Fossils, Oregon, Through Fever

Hawk's Roosting

Lying in a Hammock at William Duffy's Farm in Pine Island, Minnesota

Men at Forty

My Grandmother's Yard

Still Life

The Rain

By the end of the period, please imitate the original poem, following its pattern but using your own language. Make sure you include your name, date, and period number at the top right-hand side of your document and also include your title with an apology to the poet.

Example:

Rick Monroe
4/4/92
Per. 6

My Grandfather's Way
(with apologies to Nikki Giovanni)

I always hated my Grandfather's
rough language,

his calloused hands
He labored with
wood and
tutored me
his halting words
uttered over
fir and oak
smooth and true . . .

Figure 9. Imitating Poetry Exercise.

a drawing or piece of writing is posted, I pass out the handout in Figure 10 and set a due date for its completion.

The writing wall response sheet is important because it gives students an opportunity to hear what their peers think about their

---

From the Writing Wall

Your Name: _____

Writer's Name: _____

Title of Piece: _____

    1. What do you consider the one particular strength of this piece? Be specific, and use examples to support what you say.

    2. Recopy one sentence you find especially well written.

Figure 10. Writing Wall Response Sheet.

work, freeing me from being the primary reader/responder. I use the writing wall quite a bit. Because work is regularly posted, my students eventually get into the habit of strolling along the writing wall. They read a portion or all of a piece, and, like anyone visiting a museum or art gallery, nod or shake their heads. The writing wall sheet gives students an opportunity to talk directly to the writer/artist.

I post work from all of my classes, so my students have an expanded sense of who is participating in what I call a community of learners. I do not read or grade these responses. The value of the writing wall sheet is that another student cared enough to respond. I give each student a check mark in the gradebook for filling out a "From the Writing Wall" sheet; then I hand these sheets to the appropriate writer/artist the next day.

Imitation and the Split Screen

One of the really great features of a networked lab is the shared file. As explained earlier, networking software allows students to retrieve exemplary read-only files. Teachers can show students how to develop paragraphs or poems based on several literary works emphasizing stylistic qualities such as rhythm, assonance, complexity of syntax, or imagery.

Each student chooses one passage from a selection of three or four passages. The assignment is to create an almost literal imitation of the original passage. If you insert hard returns between the sentences in the lesson file, then students can enter their work between the lines

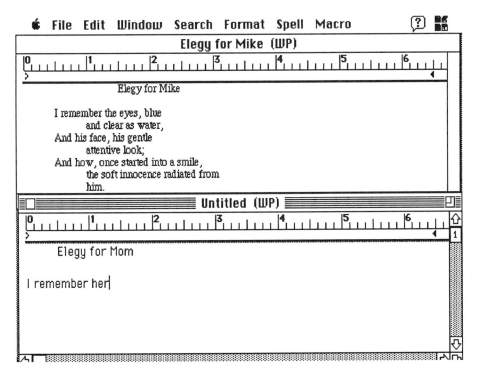

Figure 11. Split Screen.

of the original passage in a different typeface, deleting the original text when they are finished.

I like to encourage working with multiple windows as well. All a student has to do is open the lesson file he or she is going to imitate and then split the screen so the lesson file is displayed on the upper half of the screen. The student can now write his or her draft on the lower half of the screen. Figure 11 shows a split screen. Most word-processing programs include a split-screen effect.

After a student finishes the imitation, he or she can then save the work and place it in a drop folder where the teacher can then look at the piece and decide if it warrants being included in the shared Models folder. With very little effort a teacher can amass quite a collection of exemplary student models.

Many possibilities exist here for having students follow up the lesson by creating longer original pieces "in the style of. . . ." Perhaps this might serve as one of the best ways for students to get a feel for how diction, organization, or dialect affect a writer's communicative purpose.

The following is an example of what a student wrote after reading chapter 12 of *The Adventures of Huckleberry Finn*. She was not happy with imitating just one paragraph, so she extended her response.

One Night On the Ole Mississip

We was a glidin' down the river, just us two, me and Jim. We was layin' on our backs, just relaxin'. We felt like we warn't movin' a bit, but I know's we was on account a when I put my toe in the water, the water went a rushin' by my toe. It was so peaceful though, it sure felt like we warn't movin'.

I looked up in the sky. I wondered what a star would look like if I was to be lookin' at one real close. By and by, I decided they had to look happy to be so bright all the time. That night them stars sure was bright, too. It was kinda like they was all smilin' too, so we was all smilin'—I reckin we all looked like one happy bunch.

I sure did like these kind'a nights on the river. When it was just me and Jim, and the sky was as clear as it was that night, I reckin I would'a liked to stay there forever. Everything was so easy I didn't have no Miss Watson tellin' me I was a fool. I didn't have no Pap a swattin' me with them hickery. I didn't have to worry 'bout bein' civilized, nither. Yep! The ole Mississip was real nice.

I reckin if it was a person, it would'a 'bin some big, chubby, old lady. The kind with them wrinkles around the eyes from chucklin' too much, and a smile that never went away, but was there all the time. I reckin her arms would always be open too, wantin' a hug. She wouldn't be botherin' with being civilized, or educated, she just wouldn't care for that sort of thing. I think that's what the Mississip would be like. Just as friendly, and as peaceful as could be.

I was gettin' real tired 'bout then, but I didn't want to go to sleep, on account a it bein' such a nice night. I stretched and gaped and stared at the sky. I finally did fall asleep, but it warn't 'til all them stars and the moon waved to me and said good night by a twinklin' at me.

"What If" and the Business Letter

This assignment came out of my frustration with all the rhetoric about the failure of schooling in America. I have used this lesson with

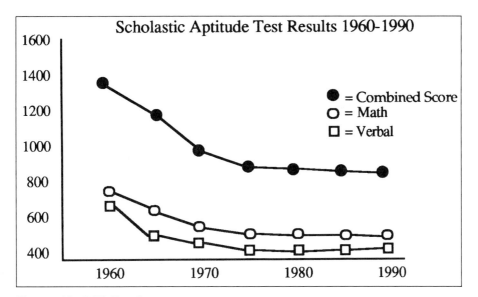

Figure 12. SAT Graph.

sophomores during the trimester they take speech, elaborating on the original writing assignment so that students actually conduct the interview and develop a portfolio of their work, which includes the business letter.

Quite a bit of research goes into this activity. Students take an interest inventory survey supplied by our career counselor that helps them identify three careers suited to their temperaments. Afterward, they study the interest inventory booklet to see what kind of additional training and schooling is required. It is a sobering moment for most students when they see what it takes to become an architect or a veterinarian. Our career counselor provides the resources students will need to find schools that offer programs they are interested in, and while this general research is going on, I prepare students for the business letter they will write. But I am getting ahead of myself. Let me return to the beginning and re-create the scenario.

Realizing that immersing students in an elaborate context produces clearer, more detailed, and meaningful writing, I show them the graph in Figure 12 and ask them to interpret it, writing in their learning logs what it says to them.

After ten minutes of freewriting, I ask students to read their initial responses to the members of their writing group. Then, on the overhead projector, I show students a few brief excerpts taken from newspapers and magazines that decry the decrepit state of education in the United States. All of these articles attack the educational system, saying that students cannot read, write, or compute.

Having created a suitable tone, I say, "Imagine if the government decided to act on the recommendations provided by the Commission on Excellence in Education. What if at the end of this year all students had to submit to rigorous testing and interviewing so that only the best, the brightest, the most industrious, and the most committed received the education this rich country is capable of providing?"

I ask students to think how their attitudes about school might be different if in August all students underwent a battery of tests that measured academic progress and potential. And suppose that, after testing, interviews were set up between students, their parents, and a committee from the school they hoped to attend. What if potential schools asked students for a portfolio that included the following:

1. all grades and test scores compiled throughout schooling;

2. a list of athletic, artistic, social, and personal accomplishments;

3. a summary statement from three teachers concerning a student's academic, social, moral, and behavioral development;

4. a letter from a parent/guardian attesting to a student's background;

5. a letter from someone other than a relative confirming the student's desire to continue his or her education; and most important,

6. a letter written by the student addressed to the school's admissions committee.

Even though my students know that this is an imaginary scenario, something I concocted, they remember the newspaper and magazine excerpts I showed them; they know about the "A Nation at Risk" report.

The scene established, I tell my students that we are going to write a business letter that: (1) states reasons why they want to continue their education, (2) provides valuable information about themselves as learners. Although I only care about the letters they will write about themselves, my students demanded that we compile a portfolio that included the six items listed above. The students also suggested that we actually conduct the interviews. So that is what we did. Classmates interviewed each other, taking on these roles: concerned citizen, member of the business community, student leader, school counselor, teacher, and principal.

Woodinville High School Panel
19819 136th Ave. NE
Woodinville, WA 98072

April 1, 19xx

Dear Panel:

> Pretend this block is your first paragraph. Make sure you tell the panel what you want. Don't forget to justify your text.

> Talk about yourself in one of these paragraphs. Remember, desire is an important part of this scenario. Use Time 12 font.

> Just because there are only three blocks, don't be misled into thinking you only need to write three paragraphs. Your letter cannot exceed one page.

Sincerely,

Rick Monroe

Figure 13. Business Letter Form.

The computer came in when we began drafting the business letter. There are lots of ways to prepare students for this letter—students might cluster or freewrite, but I wanted to use the computer to encourage students to write fluently, to generate a lot of raw material. Then, they would use the computer to shape what they had to say. I wanted them to discover what they meant and this took time, so we brainstormed and then developed a set of questions they thought would help them get started. I saved these questions in a shared folder. When my students went to the networked computer lab, they logged-on and opened the "What If" lesson file, using their questions to do a focused freewrite.

Students enjoyed using these lesson files. They could safely expand ideas and compress them later. Like an accordion, these files grew and shrank as students figured out what they meant to say in their writing.

After a center of gravity has emerged and students have spent several sessions writing on and off the computer, we talk about the form of the business letter. I make an overhead transparency (see Figure 13) that replicates what they are supposed to do. Of course, after some discussion about arrangement, tone, or form, I tell my students they can open a prepared business letter template. When ready, they can open a file called "Business Letter." All they have to do then is open their draft, copy it, and paste it into the business letter template.

Creating a template for the business letter is easy to do with any computer. All you have to do is set the tabs, insert the date, return address, and closing where you want them, and justify the space where students will paste their text. And again, if you are using a local area network, you can create and save the template in a shared folder as you would any lesson file. If you are using stand-alone computers, then you will have to save the template to separate disks. Of course, you will have to hope that the first person who uses this file doesn't save his or her work over your template, something that can't happen in a networked setting.

Drawing into Narrative*

Like most of the writing my students do in our networked computer lab, this lesson gave them a chance to develop a piece of writing over time. More important, because the writing comes out of my students' experiences, these writers tend to produce more detailed and better organized pieces. Even though this lesson was originally used with basic sophomores, my most reluctant writers, the final products were titled and averaged two-and-a-half double-spaced pages. The greatest success came after we finished, because many of these students wanted to continue working on their stories or wanted to write a series of autobiographical incidents. Clearly, there is nothing more enticing than telling your own story.

The assignment has several parts. To start, I give students the following prompt:

> Think about an experience important to you for some reason.
> Draw what happened. Include action and more than one person.
> (This provides the framework for future dialogue.)

Remember, the first time I did this, I tried it with my most reluctant writers. Our networked computer lab is large enough to include about

---

* This lesson was originally written by Jessica Hohman Halliday, my student teacher, and me. It was published in *The English Classroom in the Computer Age: Thirty Lesson Plans* (NCTE, 1991). Its format has been slightly adapted and expanded for this book.

twenty desks in the center of the room; the computers face the exterior walls. After doodling in their learning logs at the desks in the center of the lab, these students moved to the computers. Remember, inexperienced writers need to talk through their ideas. I allowed them that freedom.

At the computer, students loaded SuperPaint or Art RoundUP (a simple drawing accessory) and drew their autobiographical experiences. These sophomores had no prior experience with drawing or painting programs. They were familiar with the computer environment, however, because they had been writing with Microsoft® Works 2:00a twice a week for a month. Students experimented with the graphics program of their choice for one class period. The next day, they drew and printed their autobiographical incidents.

These students started and finished this assignment in the networked computer lab because they were reluctant writers. With my more willing students, I have them draw their experiences in their learning logs, using colored pencils or crayons while listening to some kind of instrumental music.

After drawing their experiences, students meet in writing groups for about twenty minutes and talk about their pictures, explaining what they have drawn, telling the stories their pictures represent. Then they begin drafting on the computer the stories they told their writing groups. These students worked on this particular piece twice a week over ten weeks.

Depending on the students, teachers can either set a due date or they can establish a writing routine. For example, with my reluctant writers, Monday and Wednesday were writing days in the computer lab. On one of these days, students worked on their writing by themselves. On the second day, I consulted with students: I asked them questions about their writing; I showed them how to punctuate dialogue; I showed them how to use the spell checker, the cut-and-paste option, and any other features they might need to develop the piece. It is important to establish some kind of routine for students to follow. As I said in the introduction, all of my students meet once a week in our networked computer lab to work on their polished pieces.

In considering this lesson, keep in mind that drawing is an excellent way to help students discover a way into and out of literature. Because drawing is metaphorical, it will be difficult for students at first. However, if you don't restrict them too much and especially if you don't give them too many directions, students will surprise themselves. For example, while reading *A Wizard of Earthsea* I asked my sophomores to draw what they thought was crucial in the novel. I did not ask them to draw the plot or the theme, and certainly I did not ask them to draw anything as mundane as a portrait of Ged. The point was to have them decide what was important and then find some way to express it as art. Students naturally had to choose symbols that represented what they meant. After four or five days, students were able to talk about what they had drawn because their subconscious wills continued probing what their hands had started.

Exploring any text this way takes time because it is intuitive. The mind has a tendency to make and see meaning in text, whether musical, visual, or written; but, like remembering the names of strangers, we must first become familiar with a text before we invest too much energy in it. It's difficult to remember that, unlike us, students haven't read a novel fifteen times; they haven't thought about the characters, the historical moment, or the themes. To expect students to re-create in their drawings what teachers have labored to acquire over multiple readings of a text is unfair. Students will, if given time, construct meaningful relationships among themselves, the literature, and their drawings.

Making Connections with Clip Art

Andy Hegeman, a colleague at Woodinville High School, used clip art and song lyrics to help his students re-see a text. Like me, Andy recognized that making connections between texts and pictures was a valuable way to help students build bridges between their interpretations of texts they had read and their interaction with those texts afterward. Andy's lesson uses the same principles as "Drawing into Narrative." The primary difference, and this is significant, is that students do not draw pictures that illustrate how they see the text. Instead, they use clip art available in the networked computer lab.

The procedures are simple. Ask students to bring lyrics to one of their favorite songs the next time they meet in the lab. On that first day, students enter and save the lyrics in their shared class folder. Next, show students how to access and use the clip art. Within ten minutes, students can learn to survey the clip art, look for pictures associated with their songs, and copy and paste these pictures next to the lyrics they entered earlier.

Besides being fun, this activity helps students realize that they need to read meaning into the clip art as well as the song lyrics. Everyone reads meaning into situations, conversations, and pictures;

and this exercise helps the visually oriented student make literal and figurative connections. Unlike "Drawing into Narrative," this exercise is primarily a reading assignment, but it reveals quite a bit about a student's ability. For example, some students might choose graphics that are literal while others might select and adapt graphics that are figurative. A teacher can learn quite a bit about a student based on his or her juxtaposition of pictures and text.

It is important for students to have the opportunity to make meaning, to interact with the text as they understand it, so the clip art chosen highlights both the author's meaning and the student's inter-action. Students print the songs with the clip art after both parts are merged. When they are back in class, ask students to write about why they chose the graphics they did. Ask students to explain how they think the clip art is associated with the lyrics. I like the recursiveness of this activity. Students read the text and then search for clip art that reflects their interaction with that text. Once the graphic is merged with the text, a student must decide if it is appropriate. Students can add different clip art or draw their own pictures as their understanding of a text changes.

Although this lesson uses text and pictures not created by students, merging text and graphics requires analysis. The selections students make reveal their varying abilities to make metaphorical connections and to build bridges of understanding between one kind of text and another. This lesson could easily be extended to include poems or excerpts from novels or stories and saved in a shared folder on a network. I think it is especially important that students do some talking and writing about what they did in this lesson. They need to realize that meaning is negotiated, that it resides between them and what they are "reading."

Writing and Responding to Literature

It should be obvious that I think about what my students and I do in the computer lab as a beginning, a prelude to something else. That something else is using computers to help students discover, develop, and articulate their thoughts. Nothing new there; my guess is that many teachers have been doing this without the assistance of a computer. For me, the biggest hurdle in helping my students take control of their learning has almost melted away, because now they don't have to start over every time they want to dress an idea in new clothes.

Using computers has done more for me than for my students. Technology has freed me from narrow thinking. Writing and thinking with a computer makes me feel generous and expansive; and that attitude has crept into my teaching, because I know we can always return to the computer lab and extend or recast our thoughts so they represent our current understanding. Donald Graves and James Moffett have been telling us for a long time that students should select their own subjects, knowing full well that, if we are paying attention, our students will choose what they need to learn. Generally, it was only the courageous who acted on this kind of generosity of spirit until reliable and easy-to-learn word-processing programs came along. And now that schools are installing computer labs, I expect teachers will change their teaching styles. I suspect the technical possibilities of the simplest computer will eventually wear down the psychological resistance all of us have when we attempt to create something.

I am sure that I know my students better because we regularly write and think with computers. Students call me over to look at their screens, to read and talk about what they are doing, and it is during these conversations that I feel like a guide and a consultant. It's an odd feeling at first, because teaching in a computer lab means abandoning presentation teaching and adopting individual teaching. Working with students in a computer lab forces teacher and student into conversations about the ideas taking shape on the screen. There is something tenuous about these conversations; they're provisional and democratic. And that blinking cursor certainly underscores the ephemeral nature of the text being discussed.

Writing in a computer lab gives us all a sense of possibilities. It's difficult to know where to start, so here are some more beginnings I use with my own students. I call them beginnings because they launch students, but that is all they are meant to do. The activities outlined below might spark some additional thinking, giving you and your students something to talk about.

The Postcard Story

The postcard story is a good beginning activity once students know how to log-on, open a new file, and save and print their work. I like to have students save their work in the shared class folder on the network, print their stories, and bring them to class the next day for an oral read-around. There are always a few lines in the stories worth further effort, and students will point them out. Students are encouraged to borrow lines they like from other files. Because we save these beginnings in a shared class folder, anyone in the class can access the file to copy intriguing lines for later development. I have had students continue their stories, transforming them into poems, or writing something new, extending these initial pieces based on all or a part of the postcard story.

1. After students log-on, ask them to type a sentence that would be a great opener for a story.

2. Allow students five minutes to read what others have written, shopping around the computer lab for an opening line they like.

3. Direct each student to sit down at the computer displaying his or her favorite sentence. Then tell them that they are supposed to write a story that culminates with this sentence. In other words, this first line will become the last line of their story.

4. Tell students that the story cannot exceed 99 words. The word limit is important, because it requires revising with a vengeance.

The Collaborative Story

The collaborative story can turn into an organizational Charybdis, so it is important to make sure students are clear about the procedures. It is a good idea to set five separate due dates, so the group members know when their additions should be completed. I require the group member who made the most recent addition to save the file using both the filename and the current date. That way, the other members of the group will know when their story was last altered.

A networked lab makes this activity easier to organize, but it can be done using stand-alone computers without hard drives. Teachers will have to do some additional planning, however. First of all, you'll need to provide clearly labeled disks with the group name, names of students, or some identifying number on each disk. If each group is using its own disk, then you'll need as many disks as there are groups, about twenty-five to thirty. The disks will have to be stored in the computer lab so that all group members will have access to them during the day. If your computer lab has hard drives, then stations will have to be numbered and a group folder will have to be established on each computer's hard drive. Group I uses computer one and so on. This will eliminate the confusion of groups accidentally adding to a story that isn't theirs. Of course, the more comfortable students are with the machines, the less you have to be involved in the management of files and disks. This is an important point. As teachers, our plates are already full, so anything we can do to pre-organize computer use will save us time later.

I do not grade these collaborative stories. Working with others is its own reward, especially if students are given time to share the story with the rest of their peers.

1. Break students up into groups of five, and tell them that they are going to write a collaborative story over three weeks. One member of the group logs-on and writes the beginning. I like to mix age groups and classes, so I create the groups. An easy way to do this, avoiding the organizational nightmare this activity could create, is simply to pair up students from each class by using attendance records or the gradebook. For example, the first group might be made up of the first person from each class listed in a teacher's attendance record.

2. The person who starts the story saves it over the network in a shared folder only that group has access to. Remember, creating shared folders requires that a group must be created over the network. It's a good idea to locate and name the folder so the group can easily find it. For example, because these students are in my classes, I put this new folder inside the Monroe folder. When they open the Monroe folder, inside it are the Assignments folder, class folders, and the new multi-writer group folders. I give these multi-writer folders simple names, such as MWS Group I, MWS Group II, and so forth. Creating limited-access shared folders within free-access shared folders takes some planning, so make sure you review the networking administration handbook before attempting this. Of course, to make the entire process simpler, you could make the multi-writer group folders accessible to everyone. Security is the only worry then.

3. My students meet in the computer lab at least once a week. When they log-on, I instruct them to open their group folders, read the file the first member already started, and then add to it. Because the primary point is to have fun and break down the artificial barriers of periods and class titles, I ask group members to spend not much more than ten minutes adding to the stories. The rest of the time is spent working on their polished pieces. (See the introduction for a discussion of the polished piece.)

4. I set a final due date within three weeks. That usually means students will have to go to the lab before or after school or during their lunch breaks to add to the group stories.

5. The last writer must create a semi-plausible ending. When the stories are completed, each group prints out their story and

we either post them on the writing wall or spend a day conducting a read-around.

Questioning Each Other and a Text

I routinely ask students to interact with a text by writing questions they need answered in their learning logs. Generally, we pass the learning logs to others in the class and speculate about the answers. This kind of listening and responding activity is easily adapted for use in a networked computer lab. As an extension of their learning logs, all I do is create a new file inside the Assignments folder, calling it "Questions about *Hamlet*" or whatever we happen to be reading at the time. As questions are generated in their learning logs, students go to the computer lab and add their most pressing question(s) to the "Questions about . . ." file. It doesn't take long to generate a list. What's useful about this kind of file is that students see that others have similar questions. This is a nonthreatening way to encourage a community of learners.

Maintaining this kind of electronic response log is simple. The procedures are the same as establishing any kind of lesson file in a networked lab. Again, if you are using stand-alone computers, separate and clearly labeled disks are desirable. I use the following steps when creating an electronic learning log:

1. During and after reading a story, poem, or part of a novel, ask students to write questions they need answered in their learning logs.

2. During and immediately after their first reading of the text, students might ask questions about their initial impressions or dominant images.

3. After the second reading, students generate three to six questions they need answered. These will prompt discussion later.

4. Ask students to type their most compelling questions in a file called "Questions about. . . ." Be sure to give them a due date. It's a good idea not to allow too much time to elapse when students are reading short texts. Remember, this is a folder everyone has access to, a folder students can open and save their questions in.

5. After the questions have been generated, ask students to select and copy five questions. Tell them to open a new word-processing file, paste their questions into it, and answer them. This activity constitutes prewriting for later class discussion. It is important to stress that students do not have to know the "right" answers to these questions; they need only be willing to explore possible responses.

6. Have students save their responses and print them. There are several avenues you might take now. Students could meet in writing groups and read their responses, choosing one they want to share with the entire class. You might conduct a read-around of one response per student. Or students might post the questions and accompanying responses on the writing wall. I like to conduct a Quaker Read-Around. (See More about Lesson Files and Shared Folders for a description of the Quaker Read-Around.)

Writing about Literature

The activities explained here can be done within one class or across age groups. The idea is to create a detailed scenario much like the one discussed in the "What If" and the Business Letter lesson, except this one is centered on a situation that comes out of a work of literature read by the whole class or by a smaller group. I like using these writing-to-learn prompts, because they help students re-create some aspect of the text. You could use them as alternatives to book reports, starters for class discussion, or you could ask students to extend and blend their responses into some writing exercise that is more formal.

Possible scenarios might be:

- You are Mathu (from *A Gathering of Old Men*) squatting on the front garry watching the developments of the afternoon. Write an interior monologue about what you are thinking. Use this to open an essay in which you discuss, from your point of view, what you had Mathu think.

- Develop an analogy between something in the course material and something that exists in your room, house, mind, locker, etc.

   Example: If Macbeth were a weapon, he would be a . . . because . . .

- Put yourself in the place of someone who does not exist within the text but does exist within the time period of the text.

   Example: George (from *Of Mice and Men*) and an eager Adolf Hitler discuss how to attain one's dreams.

- Create a conversation between two characters. One character may be from another text or the second voice may be you speaking to a character in the text.

   Example: Willy Loman and his brother Ben sit together on the Loman back porch.

The goal of this exercise is to invent conversation that might be exchanged by two people who are talking through ideas and events that must be understood in order to appreciate some aspect of the course material. Each student drafts an initial response to the assignment in the computer lab. Then two to three consulting readers, preferably from the student's writing group, respond to the draft using a different font. They talk back to the student, extending what the student has written or making specific suggestions to play the believing and doubting game Peter Elbow explains in *Writing Without Teachers*. The writer(s) can then print out the comments and suggestions and review them, taking them into consideration while drafting and revising.

One clear advantage to doing this activity instead of having a normal writing group session is that writer(s) have the recommendations typed on their drafts. If a suggestion is particularly insightful, the writer can, with a few keystrokes, incorporate the response into the draft, giving credit to the student who wrote it much as he or she would any other authority.

Writing-to-Learn Strategies

The measure of success in education should be how well students can think rather than how much of the teacher's knowledge they take with them as they leave class.

—Anne Gere, *Roots in the Sawdust*

I use the following writing-to-learn strategies throughout the year, requiring students to make connections in their learning logs within and beyond a text, extending the conversation begun by the course material. I do not give students these strategies in the form of a handout. Instead, I either put a strategy in the shared Assignments folder and instruct students to go to the computer lab on their own time or I write a prompt on the overhead projector, giving students ten to fifteen minutes to respond in their learning logs at the beginning of class.

- Focused Write: This is the most common kind of writing-to-learn strategy. Decide on a single element or question about the course material and ask students to discuss it. Instruct them to make one connection to themselves in the Focused Write.

  Example: Macbeth sees three witches. Are they real, or is he beginning to be . . . because . . .

- Metaphorical Question: Develop an analogy between something in the course material and something that exists in a student's bedroom, house, mind, locker, etc.

  Example: If Macbeth were a textbook, he would be . . . because . . .

■ Role-playing/First Person Account: Ask students to climb inside a character's skin in order to better understand that character's feelings, motivations, sensations, thoughts, and even dreams. Students might also put themselves in the place of someone who does not exist within the course material but does exist within the time frame of the course material.

Example: You are Lady Macbeth and you've been having nightmares. What's on your mind?

■ Role-playing/Dialogue: This strategy asks students to create a conversation between two characters. Both characters might be fictitious, or one may be the student speaking to a character.

Example: Invent a conversation between yourself and Lady Macbeth or Lady Macbeth and Ivan Boesky. Talk through ideas or events you think are important in the text.

■ Cluster/Vignette: Learning about a subject involves exploring the terminology and ideas of that subject. When students write down, arrange, connect, or use terms or ideas in a text, they are really studying, making the subject theirs. The idea behind the word cluster is to *discover relationships*. Some terms/ideas belong to certain "families" or groups of words; others are related, but the relationships aren't obvious or important until students begin experimenting with clustering. Students are free to draw lines and arrows, showing how words, concepts, and impressions are related.

Example: Cluster a word or phrase you found memorable in the text.
Afterward, write a one-page vignette that explains what you now know either about the text or the idea you saw in it. Talk about the choices you made and why you think you made these choices.

■ Admit Slip: This strategy gives everyone a chance to share feelings, ideas, and impressions anonymously. Everyone is "admitted" to the discussion about what we are reading/doing in class. Students are allowed to speak their minds without fear of the consequences. Hand out a half-sheet of paper and instruct students to write fast; ask them to talk candidly to the rest of the class about the course material.

Admit Slip Rules:

   a. anonymous

   b. on-task (students must deal with current course material)

   c. nonthreatening (in terms of language and attitude)

   d. spontaneous (no fair "rehearsing")

   e. legible (ready to be read aloud or posted around the room)

- Exit Slip: This strategy works the same way as the Admit Slip, except it is used at the *end* of a class period to summarize and review what has happened that day.

- Dialectical Notebook: The dialectical notebook lets students record questions, impressions, or thoughts about specific passages from poems, stories, plays, or other course materials. The design of the dialectical notebook is simply a spiral notebook. The open pages are folded vertically into four columns and numbered. The first column is for the catalyst, a quotation or question that begins the exchange. The second column is where the writer makes meaning—questioning, doubting, elaborating, or free associating. The third column is then filled in by the person responding, who "listens" to column two and responds in column three by questioning, doubting, and extending the initial comments. Column four can be used to extend the conversation for the original writer, or it can be used to write what he or she is thinking after considering the three previous columns. (See Electronic Read-Arounds and other Computer-Writing Strategies to see how this strategy works in a computer lab.)

Delving into a Difficult Text

A computer can encourage students to struggle with a difficult text even though they might like to surrender. Linda Clifton, another colleague from Woodinville High School, told me about her frustration with her juniors' unwillingness to stick with *Macbeth.* She didn't want to spoon-feed her students or frustrate them. After several conversations, I helped her design a lesson that required students to write a collaborative found poem based on what they thought were important passages from *Macbeth* and an analytical essay that traced their thinking as they struggled with the play. This activity is called a found poem because it is based on what students find in the text.

   I think you will find that this lesson requires students not only to use specific computer features while they are composing but also to return to the original text. I like the way the recursiveness of this lesson encourages students to help each other reinterpret their initial impressions of difficult material.

   Instead of assigning an entire text such as *Macbeth* or *The Scarlet Letter,* two typically difficult pieces most juniors read, break students up into groups of three to five and ask the groups to read one act of the play or one chapter of the book. Ask the groups to keep running notes as they read, marking any passages they find particularly intriguing. After groups have had a few days to interact with their texts, spend some time in class talking about and reading passages the groups thought were important. Patterns will emerge, and, with some guidance, students will be able to name and classify them.

When the class moves to the computer lab, instruct groups to enter passages they believe are important, reminding them to include the page numbers for citations later. Each group should save their citations using their classification names and group member initials. Save these files in a shared folder everyone in the class can access. Encourage students to inform each other when they find passages in their texts that relate to works other groups are reading.

The amount of talk this lesson generates keeps groups reading their assigned texts. A more important development, however, is that students notice patterns within the entire text, and they are drawn into chapters not originally assigned to their group. Give students enough

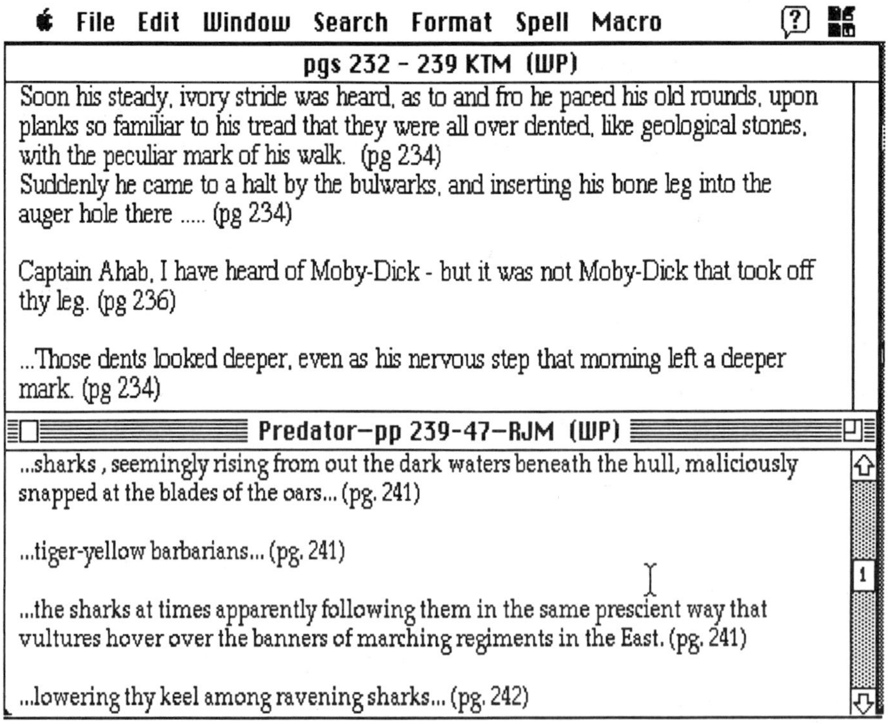

Figure 14. Split Screen 2.

time to master their section of the assigned text and several class sessions to share what each group discovered.

In her classroom, Linda Clifton took this assignment a step further. She read aloud David Wagoner's poem, "Your Fortune: A Cold Reading," as an example of how a found poem works. She told students they were going to write a found poem, using as raw material the passages the groups had entered earlier in the computer lab. Before going back to the computer lab to do this assignment, students from different groups were paired together. They were instructed to open the files their separate groups had created and then use the passages from both these files to create a collaborative found poem. Students did not have to include the page numbers from the passages as part of their poems.

Remind students to split the screen so they can bounce between both files as they write. Figure 14 shows what a split screen looks like.

I can attest to the kind of close reading students will do as they create the collaborative found poem, because during my Writing and Thinking with Computers Workshop, Linda Clifton presented an expanded version of the lesson she used with her students. The following poem was the one my partner and I created:

The Dark March
by Kathy Marion and Rick Monroe
(A found poem based on *Moby-Dick*)

This ivory leg has the better of my flesh.
    Lowering my bone leg into the dark waters
    beneath the hull,
    the shark's jaw maliciously snapped
    a deeper dent
    vulture-sharks hover
    like geological stones
    a peculiar mark.

    Those deeper dents,
    seemingly prescient,
    brought me to this ivory stride.

Moby-Dick gave me this
    deeper mark and
    nervous step.

The found poem is not the culminating activity of this lesson. After spending at least an hour cutting and pasting text and negotiating the content of their collaborative poems, students will need to bring a printout of their work to class so they can complete a series of loops (in their learning logs) designed to help them think about their previous activities. Students need to reflect often about what is asked of them, so they can begin developing problem-solving strategies they can use the next time they encounter a difficult text. The loops I assign my students might include the following:

- After your group entered the passages from the text, what else did you notice as you continued reading the text?

- As you and your partner were cutting and pasting, creating the collaborative found poem, what did you and your partner discover?

- Tell the story of your interaction with the text, including the work you did as you developed the found poem.

Because Linda wanted her students to rehearse analysis, she then asked them to write an analytical essay about the above process. The essay was written in four parts. Part one was the collaborative found poem. Part two asked students to talk about their insights and discoveries during the process of reading and searching for passages that dealt only with their group's subject. Part three required students to think about and discuss how the found poem opened up the original text. Part four asked students to talk about what seemed significant about the original text, taking into account their responses to parts one to three of the essay assignment.

Even though students were not required to use computers to draft their essays, many did so because they were then given three more weeks to complete this part of the lesson. I would have required my students to use computers to draft each of the four parts of the essay so they could spend their revising time rearranging their essays and writing transitions. I would have also asked them to use several other word-processing features to help them recast monotonous sentence patterns and search for overused words or phrases. (See Revising with a Computer in Restructuring the Classroom for Technology.) But gaining access to a computer lab isn't always possible for teachers, especially if their colleagues also need to schedule class time in the lab. It is important that the work students do be based on sound pedagogical principles. After all, your curriculum is individually designed and adjusted, and the computer is only your ally when it helps you extend the reach of that curriculum.

Extending Student Writing: The Year-End Book

One way I facilitate the idea that my students are writers is with the year-end book. During the first week of school, I assign my juniors the task of writing such a book. The basic requirements are that the books be typed or word processed; that students include a title page, and a table of contents; that they design some kind of cover art for their book; and that their book include at least one of the following kinds of writing:

[ ] Writing(s) more than a year old

[ ] Haiku (3 minimum)

[ ] Short story (yours or someone else's—1 minimum)

[ ] Literary response (learning log entry, essay, video or audio-tape, etc.)

[ ] James Moffett essay of your choice from *Active Voice*

[ ] Epitaph modeled after Ben Franklin's (1 serious and 1 humorous)

[ ] Imitation poem (based upon a poem of 15 lines or more)

[ ] Imitation of Walt Whitman's "Song of Myself"

[ ] Four other of your writings (songs, plays, essays, stories, notes to friends, wish lists, résumés; anything goes!)

[ ] Favorite quotations (5 minimum)

[ ] Selections from other authors (2 minimum)

[ ] Poetry from other authors (2 minimum)

[ ] Pictures you have taken or pictures taken by others that you like

[ ] Keepsakes (playbills, ticket stubs, cards, etc.)

[ ] Writings from other students (2 minimum)

[ ] Newspaper clippings of articles about you or about your friends or on any subject of interest to you

[ ] Your own poetry (3 minimum)

As the year progresses, students might want to also include an envelope in their writing folder to hold keepsakes and pictures, so they aren't scrambling for material near the end of the year.

It is my hope that students will do some writing they are proud of and some reading worth remembering. With this assumption in mind, my juniors and I produce this book. We use class time near the end of the year to collect it, bind it, and conduct a reading just like professional writers.

As I explained in the introduction, my students go to the computer lab at least once a week to work on assigned work, such as the sentence composing lesson file or the electronic response log, and to work on their polished pieces—writing in their chosen format. Students also use this time in the computer lab to meet in writing groups, reading their works in progress. The third trimester, I do not require a polished piece, because we are collecting, conferencing, and revising all the writing we will include in the year-end book. The computer lab makes this project feasible, because most of the students' work has been saved either on their own disks or on the network hard disk.

In addition to the year-end book, students are required to submit at least one piece of writing for publication to the school literary magazine, the school newspaper, a contest of their choice, or some other publication. Their piece need not be published, only submitted for publication.

While my colleagues are giving finals, my students select from their year-end books one or two poems or an excerpt from a longer piece and we conduct a reading. As part of the reading, students must also address, in some way, the questions listed below:

1. What was difficult?
2. What are you most pleased with?
3. What would you do differently if you had to do this project again?
4. Do you have any suggestions that could make this project easier, more fun, or more valuable?

Restructuring the Classroom for Technology

At this point, your head should be swimming with lots of ideas. You might also be reeling with confusion as you begin thinking about how to include writing and thinking lessons in a computer lab without abandoning what you currently do. In this chapter I hope to allay your fears and doubts. Truly, you do not have to be a cartoon superhero to incorporate technology into your curriculum. You will undergo some transformation; that is natural and expected any time you attempt something new. I believe that if you behave bravely, if you take that first step and use computers to write and think through problems set by you and your students, you will find your way.

It may mean that for a while you will follow your students' lead. Do not be concerned if your students know more about the mechanics of running a computer than you do. The point is that you are the learning expert; you know your discipline, so don't fret about not knowing everything there is to know about computers and programs. I suppose giving up the power associated with being "the one who knows" is often the first and most difficult adjustment many teachers have to make. After that, everything grows easier. You will find yourself changing in subtle but important ways, and you may find teaching more rewarding because you are talking to students who are actively participating in their own learning.

Not to belabor the point, let me show you how I structure my classroom. What follows is a brief discussion of a typical week.

Monday is a computer lab writing and thinking day. My students know they will always meet in our networked computer lab Mondays to work on their polished pieces. Because I use portfolio assessment in evaluating my students (See Evaluating Student Writing Equitably and Efficiently), one of the requirements they must fulfill is to write a piece they *want* to write. Students compose drafts, meet in writing groups, and continue drafting and revising poems, stories, plays, novels, and essays throughout the trimester and the year. All I do is give them the opportunity to write something they want to write. The only guideline I give to students who are writing poetry is that three poems or one lengthy poem is equivalent to one short story. I do not provide a length requirement for short stories.

So every Monday my class meets in the computer lab. The routine is important and cannot be underestimated. In the lab, half of the class writes on the computer and the other half meets in writing groups. I enter the writing groups into the computer, numbering them 1–6 (yes, I have 25–30 students in each class), and give students a copy. The first few Mondays of the trimester, we all go to the computer lab to begin drafting. I roam around the room and talk to students who are stuck or need someone to listen to them. Usually, though, I sit at a computer and write with them. And when called away from my writing, I make exaggerated huffs and puffs, making it clear that I need time to work on my own writing as well. By the third week, I have developed a fairly simple rotation. Writing groups 1–3 are at the computer, developing their polished pieces. Writing groups 4–6 are meeting in the center of the lab, conducting writing group sessions. Whenever a writing group finishes, members may move to the computer to begin revision. The next week, writing groups switch positions: groups 1–3 meet in their writing groups, and groups 4–6 work at the computers. This procedure continues until the tenth week, one week before portfolios are due.

Tuesday through Thursday are spent doing what many of us would recognize as English. Students enter class, take out their learning logs, and prepare to write about or discuss issues that emerge from what we are doing at the time. I like to establish the habit of beginning classwork right away. As students enter my class, I like to have directions on display from an overhead projector. For example, before reading *Soul Catcher*, I might display the following directions:

> Imagine we are overtaken by a foreign power. Think about the traditions and beliefs you hold sacred, those ideas you would die for if necessary. In your learning log, set the scene and then talk about the traditions and beliefs you would try to maintain. If you want to turn this into a story later, that's okay.

The next day, I put students into small groups and direct them to read the previous day's entries. This gives me time to take attendance and move around the room so I can listen to what they have to say. Thursday might be spent reading a poem thematically related to *Soul Catcher* and then responding to it via a dialectical notebook entry. In my class, Friday is a free reading day. Students are given credit for the class if they spend the period reading for fun. (See Book Reviews with FileMaker Pro.)

Revising with a Computer

Revision is a powerful lure when using a computer. I teach my students many of the features they might use while revising when we are in the computer lab. I roam around the room looking over their shoulders, consulting with students as they develop their writing. Occasionally I conduct revising seminars. On those occasions I bring the PC viewer to class and ask a student if I can use his or her file. I always use something short, such as the postcard story, because it is brief and familiar. Anyone can be easily confused or overloaded with information when revising with a computer, so, to avoid cognitive dissonance, I display only short pieces of writing during these seminar sessions. Then my students and I go to the computer lab to practice the word-processing features we experimented with the day before.

I suggest showing students one or two of the following five activities that illustrate various word-processing features:

1. Hard returns and arranging text: Open a familiar text, such as the postcard story and insert returns after each sentence so each one is isolated. This helps students see if all the sentences are complete sentences. Experiment with the arrangement of text, cutting and pasting sentences for effect.

2. Styles of type: Put the first four words of every sentence in boldface type. This calls attention to sentence openings, allowing the writer to recognize and recast repetitive patterns.

3. The find feature: Search for every occurrence of the suffixes *-ly, -ing,* and *-ed.* This is a good time to remind students they can find and replace overused or commonly misspelled words. (I require my students to note error patterns they consistently make in their learning logs. Students continue making the same mistakes until they internalize their error patterns.)

4. The spell checker: I make sure students understand that the computer cannot read; students still have to decide if what the computer flags is correct. This is especially true with homophones such as to/too/two and there/their/they're.

5. The split screen: Split the screen and remind students about accordion writing. Spend a few minutes expanding or compressing a sentence, experimenting with detail or form.

Evaluating Student Writing Equitably and Efficiently

My thinking about the evaluation of student writing has undergone some transformations over the last thirteen years. What I have to say may sound complex and even unorthodox, but it is straightforward. Evaluating a student's work means assessing growth. When I think of evaluation, I do not think about grading, because grading implies measuring discrete skills; whereas, assessing a student's ability to manipulate language in any situation for any reader is much more complex. You may object to the MAT 6, CAT, SAT, or ACT tests, but you cannot ignore their effect on you and your students. It is important, then, to question our assumptions about evaluation. Let me take a moment to make clear four of my guiding principles. They are based on the belief that I am only partly responsible for helping my students successfully understand and take control over situations in which they will use language in any context for any reader whether real or imagined.

1. I believe we are a community of thinkers and therefore need to be tentative, observant, and rigorous in our use of language.

2. I believe resisting the urge to bring closure to a piece of writing enriches the potential for articulating and extending thought.

3. I believe what students have to say is important—that they can and should learn from each other.

4. I believe students are capable of and should take part in setting criteria for assignments designed by themselves and others.

While developing your own guiding principles for evaluation, make sure they include two kinds of assessment: formative and summative. Formative evaluation is ongoing. That is, a student might complete a learning log entry or draft a poem or an essay, receiving responses about his or her work from peers *and* the teacher. The role of the teacher when conducting formative evaluation is that of mentor. The teacher does not instruct but consults, helping the student by questioning and commenting, setting up a conversation between writer and reader. Formative evaluation is important because it is tentative and fluid. The students' response to this form of evaluation, although not graded, is considered. I take careful notice of the patterns students use, helping them see the fabric of their work over the year.

Summative evaluation brings closure to a piece. In the ideal situation, students and I establish the evaluation criteria before the piece is completed and after the first round of writing groups and student/reader and student/teacher conferences. Assessment sheets keep students on track. They also help me maintain realistic expectations. I know assessment sheets are difficult to do for large numbers of students, but it is important for students to have the assessment criteria as they are developing their drafts so they can use them to guide their revising.

So, how does a teacher manage such a complex process? How do you draw on the strengths of both formative and summative evaluation? I use the project and portfolio approach.

A project I have used over the last five years is one I have talked about quite a bit in this book—the polished piece. I assign the due dates, and my students meet in writing groups throughout the trimester, helping each other develop their drafts. Over the trimester, I meet with students Mondays when we are in the computer lab and Fridays while my students are reading for fun.

The portfolio approach is similar. Students meet in writing groups several times while drafting a piece. Several weeks before the trimester is over, students select three or four pieces of their work that they want evaluated. In the past I have avoided receiving only one kind of writing by requiring a minimum of one expository essay, one poem, and one literary response, leaving the fourth selection to a student's discretion. Using the portfolio approach gives all of us more time to concentrate on the act of manipulating language, because assignments are based on form. It doesn't matter if a student writes a response to a novel as a poem or an essay. All I need to do is make sure students have had plenty of practice with multiple forms. What I haven't done in the past, and will do in the future, is to ask students to include one piece in their portfolios that they are not satisfied with. Then, we will be able to talk about what is and what is not working in their writing.

We have spent some time exercising our minds, developing a habit of mind, by rehearsing several thinking strategies. It is time to reflect about what you have learned and what you are still not sure about. That is, it is time to conduct an audit, make an accounting of your efforts and accomplishments so far.

Write me a letter, not to exceed two double-spaced typed pages, that answers the following questions:

What's in stock? What do you know now about yourself as a thinker that you didn't before?

What's on back order? What are you still unsure about? What problems are you having?

(Refer to specific incidents, drawing on your learning log entries and what has been collected in your writing folder to this point.)

Figure 15. Audit #1.

Recently, my colleague Joan Fiset and I have been working together, designing lessons, investigating resources, and talking about ways we can help students become autonomous learners. One of the resources we have found helpful as we continue to reshape how we use portfolio assessment is a text called *Mind Matters: Teaching for Thinking.* Dan Kirby, one of the book's authors, asks his students to write him a letter, a progress report, each week. He calls these status reports *audits*. I am using a form of the audit as one of the tools students can use to take responsibility for their own development as writers. This strategy is one that all of us can use as we struggle with authentic assessment.

The audit is proving a fine vehicle for my students to talk specifically about their growth. Every three weeks, I ask students to write a letter describing what they know and what they are still confused about or find unclear. As the trimester and year progress, I adjust the questions and add one or two others, but the first audit of this year dealt with two basic questions. They are represented in Figure 15.

By keeping track of their development for themselves, students begin to see that they are also responsible for considering what they know and how they have come to know it. I collect, read, and keep the audits and will bring them out for the midterm conference. In addition to the audits, a student brings his or her learning log to the conference, and the two of us sit down and talk about a few of the entries. One entry is chosen by me because it exemplifies a particular

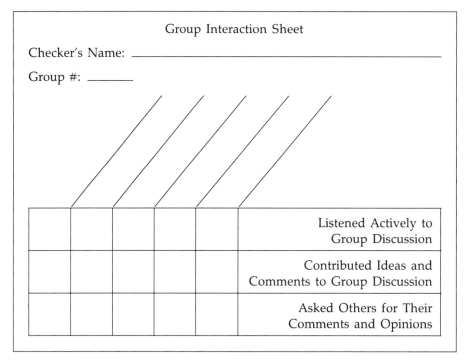

Figure 16. Group Interaction Sheet.

thinking strategy, and one is chosen by the student because of its potential for revision. When we confer later, we can extend our previous conversation. By the end of the year, each student should have an extensive paper and verbal trail showing his or her development.

I can afford to be patient because I have the same students all year. I resist the impulse to rush my students to produce several different kinds of final products. In subsequent informal conferences students sometimes bring several beginnings of drafts from their learning logs. For example, one of these beginnings might be verse or a narrative. In the conference, we might then talk about how casting a response to a novel in the form of a poem changed the student's understanding of the original text. One completed piece we might talk about is an essay the student wrote as a kind of anthropologist. The idea here is that students review their writing folders and learning logs and then describe what they know about themselves based on the accumulated artifacts. Eventually, students develop portfolios that include pieces in progress (beginnings) and pieces that are polished.

Another useful formative assessment tool that I incorporated into classwork this year is the group interaction sheet shown in Figure 16.

```
┌─────────────────────────────────────────────────────────────────┐
│                                                                   │
│   Names of Group Members:        _____   │
│                                                                   │
│                                  _____   │
│                                                                   │
│   √  What is one thing we did well?                               │
│                                                                   │
│   √  What is one thing we can work to improve next time?          │
│                                                                   │
└─────────────────────────────────────────────────────────────────┘
```

Figure 17. Group Self-Evaluation Sheet.

Joan Fiset developed it, and we both use it every time students work in groups. Like the audit, it reminds students they need to be conscious of what they are doing. It's a simple procedure. Students work in groups of five. One member is the checker, one is the coordinator, and another is the recorder. The checker writes the names of the group members along the diagonal lines at the top of the sheet and then puts a check mark in the appropriate boxes when a member adds to their group effort. The checker doesn't talk; instead, he or she observes and records the dynamics of the group. The coordinator invites the other members to participate, making sure everyone contributes and has some level of investment in the group's work. The recorder drafts the group's work. If the goal is to write a collaborative poem, the recorder is responsible for writing out what the group negotiates. After all group work, the recorder fills out a group self-evaluation sheet (see Figure 17), noting what went well and what needs improvement.

The recorder collects both sheets, staples them together, and hands them in. I look them over, reading for information I didn't detect while I was moving in and out of the groups. A few students will always ask if their group earned an A. Tell these students that both sheets are tools, reminders of what they should be doing when they are working with others. Joining a community of thinkers requires vigilance.

Obviously, there is more to assessment than grading. I hope you will be encouraged to struggle with the guiding principles you use to inform your approach to assessment. By doing so, you might find that you will begin thinking of yourself as a mentor and an observer instead of an evaluator and a critic. I am positive you will find that by postponing summative evaluation, you and your students will have time to exchange ideas. In my class, that process is producing students who are becoming autonomous evaluators of their own thinking.

Additional Thoughts

About four weeks into the first trimester, after my students and I have gotten to know one another, we begin negotiating what will be included in their portfolios. Up to this point, we've been learning and rehearsing strategies for thinking as it relates to writing, reading, and drawing. I have not evaluated their work using letter grades, points, or percentages, because I want my students to be comfortable immersing themselves in the thinking process. It is important to create a supportive atmosphere, or students will not take the risks necessary for growth.

My aim is for us to work together as a community of writers and thinkers, stretching our minds and gaining new skills students will value the rest of their lives.

When it is time to collect and assess the students' work, I provide some general guidelines, and my students decide which pieces they want to include in their portfolios. The first trimester, I ask students to include at least the following:

1. A piece of writing that has progressed from an early draft into a finished piece. It can be prose or poetry. The student should include all drafts as well as suggestions from their writing group. The student should include acknowledgments—the names of people who offered helpful feedback.

2. Samples of writing that reflect five "habits of mind" (e.g., probative, analytic, poetic/narrative, visual, and reflective) excerpted from a student's writing folder and/or learning log. (The habits of mind are defined later.)

3. A final audit letter—students review and report on what they have learned, using detailed examples to support and illustrate their claims. The final audit should not exceed two double-spaced typed pages.

As you can see, there is still room for the students to make choices. In addition to the written record, we talk about the goals of the class and how we might assess the following:

■ Your overall contribution as a member of the entire classroom community: your willingness to participate, listen, and cooperate as observed by me.

■ Collaborative work in reading, writing, and core groups as observed by peers and me.

■ Evidence that you have sustained inquiry by handing in all your work, maintaining your learning log and drawings.

Because I watch my students, paying more attention to them than they do to me, I can generally assess a student's contribution to our community. I make brief notes in my gradebook each week or when students are meeting in writing groups. I note who is prepared and who has actively contributed with a check mark. Students who are not prepared or who do not help their peers receive a zero. I also make use of any extra moments I have in class to comment on or praise individuals for their level of participation. By the fourth week, my students know I am concerned and involved in their learning.

The more informal types of writings we do, electronic learning log entries, electronic response logs, and reactions to others' informal entries, are evaluated primarily by quantity. Students earn a check mark if they have met the minimum weekly number of required entries and have written a respectable amount in these entries: from a paragraph to a page. Relevance and weightiness might also be evaluated if you have the time to make spot-checks of entries. Generally, I don't want to read my students' learning log entries, because I believe students need a place they can experiment with thought without judgment. We make time later to develop those initial thoughts.

Assessing a student's collaborative effort is simple because all I have to do is review the group interaction sheets. I keep these in a folder and allow students to look at them whenever they want. These sheets are useful reminders to me and to my students. They are records of what actually happened on a given day versus how we remember what happened. Memory is a slippery thing, and all of us need to look at the facts when we cast back and reflect about our efforts.

I mentioned students needed to include excerpts of particular kinds of thinking, what Anne Berthoff, Paul Connolly, and others refer to as "habits of mind." Students label samples of various habits of mind they have photocopied from their learning logs. Then they write a brief comment explaining how or why the samples are probative, narrative/poetic, analytic, visual, or reflective. Students decide which learning log entries they want to use. What I care about here is that my students begin to see that we have been thinking about issues from new perspectives. We have identified problems or raised questions, and then we have walked around them, examining them from multiple angles. The list below defines the five habits of mind* I want my students to include in their portfolios.

———————

* These definitions of ways of thinking were developed in the Bard College Writing and Thinking Institute, primarily by Paul Connolly (1991). Joan Fiset, a colleague of mine, is one of the Institute's instructors, and she encouraged me to include Connolly's definitions as part of my students' portfolios.

- The habit of probative thinking: Writing that explores, tests, and discovers what is felt or thought. Consider fragments or reflections you value because they begin to extend thinking in ways not yet fully understood.

- The habit of narrative/poetic thinking: Writing to tell stories or to compose poems; writing that enables people to think and to express themselves in ways analytic prose cannot.

- The habit of analytic thinking: Writing that responds to a text; writing used to think about and extend the conversation begun by other authors. Writing that explains why others think as they do and then justifies claims that support or refute the conversation someone else began.

- The habit of visual thinking: Drawing that conveys the meaning of a poem, story, or idea. Visual thinking is metaphorical; imagery provides the sense the student has of the text.

- The habit of reflective thinking: Writing to investigate self-consciously how one writes and thinks. (This metacognitive writing may be in the form of the final audit letter.)

It is important for students and teachers to negotiate the assessment criteria. Now that you have seen what is expected for my student's first trimester portfolio, I have included a few sample criteria sheets my students and I have developed over the past five years. I am currently re-thinking my use of the criteria sheet, and I may abandon it altogether. I expect that writing audits, sharing student and professional models, and conducting brief but timely conferences may not require the kind of global and analytic approach to assessment that criteria sheets imply.

The portfolio criteria sheet in Figure 18 is one my students and I used during the 1991–92 school year. As an assessment tool, it seemed to allow for a multi-dimensional view of a student's progress. I am sure next year my students and I will reshape and transform it so that the criteria sheet will be reflective of who we are and what we are doing then.

I used the portfolio criteria sheet shown two years ago with basic sophomores whom I taught over the course of a year. The last trimester, we worked on one optional topic paper and two essays—one autobiographical in nature and one as a response to Ursula K. Le-Guin's *A Wizard of Earthsea*. It should be noted that students had conferences with me and their readers at least three times on each piece during the trimester.

Portfolio/Course Evaluation Criteria

Audit Letter:
The Habit of Reflective Thinking   weak   strong

Uses detailed examples to
support and illustrate what you say.

Explores how or why your
examples are important.

Investigates your sense
of how you think.

Contribution to Our Learning Community

Contributed ideas and comments
to group discussion.

Asked others for their
comments and opinions.

Willingness to listen when
your attention is needed.

Effort in Sustaining Inquiry

All work submitted on time.   no _____ yes _____

All learning log entries complete.   no _____ yes _____

Polished Piece(s).

Your polished piece reflects a willingness to take risks, to say something
authentic. The piece is clearly done with care.

|——————————————————————————————|

beginning   in places   arrived

Is the polished piece ready to be submitted for publication?

                                        not yet _____ yes _____

Figure 18. Portfolio Criteria Sheet.

Grade	Portfolio Criteria
A	This collection showed care. Your polished piece showed imagination and used details to develop the scene and mood you wanted to convey. The essays included important supporting facts, examples, and reasons to make your points. All of the pieces hung together; they did not jump around. The sentences were properly structured and used a pattern that was not repetitive. There may have been a few spelling or usage mistakes, but overall, they did not get in the way of your meaning. What you had to say was interesting.
B	This collection showed care. Your polished piece used details to develop the scene and mood you wanted to convey. The essays included supporting facts, examples, and reasons to make your points. Most of the pieces hung together; they did not jump around. The sentences were properly structured, but you need to pay attention to variety in your sentence patterns. There were a few spelling or usage mistakes, but overall, they did not get in the way of your meaning. What you had to say was interesting.
C	This collection of writing needed to show more care. Your polished piece needed more details to develop the scene and mood you wanted to convey. The essays used some supporting facts, examples, or reasons, but you still need to think about and explain how they support your topics. Some of the pieces seemed a bit fragmented; that is, they seemed loosely constructed. Some of the sentences needed a subject or a verb to make them complete. The spelling or usage mistakes do not get in the way of your meaning, but they do detract from your meaning. What you had to say was clear.
D	This collection of writing did not show the kind of care expected given the amount of time and help available. Your polished piece could use more detail, because as it reads now, you tell more than show. The essays use some supporting facts, examples, or reasons, but they were not well thought out. The spelling or usage mistakes get in the way of your meaning, making it difficult to stay interested in your writing.

The Great Gatsby Critical Essay Criteria

The issue identified in the response is . . .

|——————————|——————————|——————————|——————————|
important.   insignificant.

Your response includes an important quotation from the text that supports/highlights your issue.

|——————————|——————————|——————————|——————————|
yes   no

You have made a connection beyond the text that seems . . .

|——————————|——————————|——————————|——————————|
thoughtful.   trivial.

The response builds bridges between the issues, the quotations, and the connections beyond the text that are . . .

|——————————|——————————|——————————|——————————|
forceful.   weak.

Comments:

You might consider . . .

The parts that kept me most interested were . . .

The part about . . . reminded me of . . .

Figure 19. Sample Essay Criteria Form.

The criteria sheet in Figure 19 was developed by my students and me as a guide while drafting a critical essay in response to *The Great Gatsby*. We applied it later in the writing process as well, making sure the writing group members and the writer understood the minimal requirements. The idea here is to develop qualitative terms that describe features important to the writing task. Remember, the more generic the criteria, the harder it is for students to take control of their writing.

The criteria sheet shown in Figure 20 is a dichotomous scale my students and I developed for a business letter. The scenario was fairly complex, but, basically, students had to write a letter to a panel convincing its members to allow them to continue school after tenth

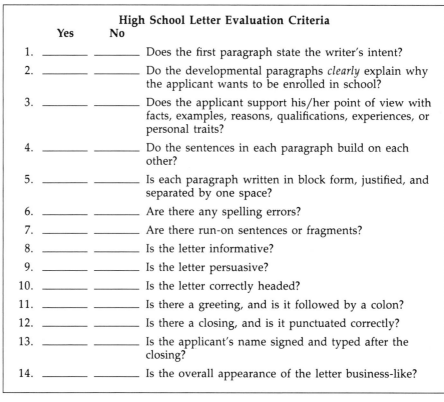

High School Letter Evaluation Criteria

	Yes	No	
1.	_____	_____	Does the first paragraph state the writer's intent?
2.	_____	_____	Do the developmental paragraphs *clearly* explain why the applicant wants to be enrolled in school?
3.	_____	_____	Does the applicant support his/her point of view with facts, examples, reasons, qualifications, experiences, or personal traits?
4.	_____	_____	Do the sentences in each paragraph build on each other?
5.	_____	_____	Is each paragraph written in block form, justified, and separated by one space?
6.	_____	_____	Are there any spelling errors?
7.	_____	_____	Are there run-on sentences or fragments?
8.	_____	_____	Is the letter informative?
9.	_____	_____	Is the letter persuasive?
10.	_____	_____	Is the letter correctly headed?
11.	_____	_____	Is there a greeting, and is it followed by a colon?
12.	_____	_____	Is there a closing, and is it punctuated correctly?
13.	_____	_____	Is the applicant's name signed and typed after the closing?
14.	_____	_____	Is the overall appearance of the letter business-like?

Figure 20. Letter Criteria Sheet.

grade. Anyone not allowed to continue with high school was inducted into the armed services or assigned community service work for two years. (See "What if" and the Business Letter for a full explanation of the scenario.)

2 Establishing a Networked Computer Lab

The Basics

A Local Area Network (LAN) is a computer lab controlled by a central computer called a file server. What makes a networked lab different from a stand-alone computer lab is that separate computer stations can electronically share information through the file server.

A school system that is considering purchasing a file server will need to think about cost and speed. Originally, Woodinville High's LAN was driven by a computer with an internal 40-megabyte hard disk. All programs were launched from this central file server, and an additional external 40-megabyte hard disk was used for storing files. Now, of course, I would purchase an additional hard disk of at least 240 megabytes. But in 1989, when I piloted the first local area network for our district, memory and computers were costly. In the spring of 1992, we upgraded our networked lab. Now the workstations have hard disks. Programs are launched from the individual computers and files are stored and shared on the file server and external hard disk.

When your school is ready to invest in a networked computer lab, I suggest purchasing a fast file server. I also suggest purchasing the largest capacity hard disk you can afford for storing and sharing files. When sharing files, especially if you plan to do any cross-curricular work, students can easily use up to 40 megabytes of storage in one trimester.

It is also important to remember that students are limited by a computer's internal memory (RAM). Purchase the most advanced computer station you can get, because you will eventually outgrow it. There is nothing more demoralizing than being stuck with computers that cannot grow with you and your students.

Having workstations with hard disks is important because all programs can be launched from these hard disks, saving valuable time. The network can then be used for what it was intended—sharing files. When I piloted Woodinville High School's LAN, I asked my colleagues what they preferred: thirty workstations or fifteen workstations with hard disks. I was limited by the district's budget and had to make a difficult choice. I preferred having the better machines (i.e., the ones with hard disks), but my colleagues made it clear they wouldn't use the computer lab unless they could take their entire class to the lab.

Old habits die hard. For several years, I had been using small groups so that I could spend more time with individual students. One day a week, half of my students worked on computers developing a piece of writing while the other half met in writing groups. The next week, the groups switched. This rotation continued for ten weeks, as students drafted and revised what I call the polished piece. Although I tried to convince my colleagues of the value of such a system, many saw it as troublesome, an additional burden in an already hectic school day. Because I could only afford fifteen workstations with hard disks, I purchased thirty without hard disks and then bought an additional external hard disk for storing files.

The decision to purchase computers without hard disks meant that programs had to be launched from the file server to the workstations, and, as you can imagine, loading 30 computer workstations with Microsoft Works over a network takes time. But we made it work. Students got in the habit of arriving early, logging-on, and opening the applications they needed for the work they were going to do that day.

I purchased a laser printer instead of several dot matrix printers because laser printers are durable and quiet. Occasionally, a teacher might want to teach half a class while the other half works at the computer. Printing on a dot matrix printer precludes any conversation. In fact, three years later, our laser printer is still working beautifully. We also purchased spooling software. Such software allows students and teachers to print a document to disk quickly; it frees the computer so the user can continue working while files are being printed.

As for applications, I purchased only software that could be used or adapted across the disciplines. I am not interested in buying software that limits what I want to teach or what my students want to learn. I believe strongly that computers should be used to do something, to solve problems, to explore thought, to extend the conversation begun in class, to create a community of learners and thinkers. I do not recommend buying prepackaged commercial learning programs (commonly known as Integrated Learning Systems), because they tend to be little more than electronic workbooks. That is not to say that I am against purchasing programs such as Writer's Helper or Correct Grammar. I think of such software in the same way I do a handbook on style or a thesaurus—if used judiciously, they are useful tools. Therefore, the following applications are currently used over Woodinville's networked computer lab:

1. Microsoft Works, because of its integrated package
2. SuperPaint, because of its painting and drawing capabilities
3. Expressionist, because it allows students to use math formulas with the computer (Now that we have hard disks for each workstation, we would purchase Mathematica or Theorist, two powerful math programs.)
4. Pagemaker, for the literary arts magazine and newspaper
5. Excel and Microsoft Word, for more sophisticated individual users
6. FileMaker Pro (an incredible database)
7. ArtRoundUP (a fine clip art and painting accessory)

To review, this is what an application-based networked computer lab requires:

1. A fast computer to act as a file server
2. An additional hard disk for storing and sharing files
3. Thirty computer workstations
4. Phone net connectors, one for each workstation so they can be networked to each other and the file server
5. Application software (See the above list, and include e-mail as well if you can afford it.)
6. Networking and print spooling software
7. A laser printer (Don't forget to purchase at least nine laser printer cartridges.)
8. Phone net wire to link the workstations together, along with the printer and the file server. (I suggest having an electrician install a backbone to prevent unnecessary crashes. Unless hardwired, the entire network can be shut down if the phone net connector from one workstation is disconnected while the network is running.)
9. A room with adequate space and power

Strengths of a Local Area Network

The primary advantage of a local area network over stand-alone computer stations is the ability to share files across the curriculum, something that is challenging and potentially enriching for students and teachers alike. Shared folders can be established so students can send each other files over the network. This is particularly useful for group work. In a networked computer lab, students no longer need to be in the same class to collaborate on a project. Once the network is up and running, it manages itself, requiring very little attention.

Weaknesses of a Local Area Network

Initially, a local area network requires quite a bit of time to set up. Because I was not sure how much time it would take, I asked colleagues for names of students who would like to participate as Technology Assistants. Their role was to learn as much as they could about programs and provide assistance to all users. Technology Assistants (TAs) also explored the limits of the file-server software.

Although the TAs were invaluable in maintaining the LAN, it is important that school districts recognize that not every school has students who are technologically advanced enough to smoothly operate an LAN. *Obviously, a supervisor should be hired or several teachers freed from teaching one or two classes to maintain the LAN and assist teachers and students.*

The other limitations pertain to hardware and software. Saving files created with any sophisticated painting or drawing application is slow over a network. To speed up file management, the file server should have at least 8 megabytes of RAM. Of course, school districts can avoid these limitations by purchasing the most advanced workstations and file server available.

Managing a Local Area Network

Because I previously managed a stand-alone lab, I relied on prior experience in setting up a local area network. This section describes what I did and what you might do when you set up your networked computer lab.

As I said, one of the first things I did was ask colleagues for names of students who could serve as Technical Assistants. A list of twenty-five students was generated, and after interviewing each candidate, I chose fifteen students. I held two meetings with potential TAs to explain their roles and responsibilities.

In addition, Dave Jones, my principal, and our counseling department set up a special credit system for these students. Each TA received independent study credit in any subject they worked with in the LAN. This insured a diverse and highly qualified group of young men and women. It is important to note, however, that students were not given credit for courses required by the state or the district.

Technical Assistants

The following outline describes the roles and responsibilities of technical assistants and some of the tasks they performed.

1. TAs are responsible for formatting disks, preparing worksta-tions when they are altered, and making sure the LAN runs smoothly.

2. TAs serve as experts for the network and the software. They are expected to troubleshoot system errors, so students and teachers can use the LAN efficiently.

3. TAs may be required to launch programs for the next class.

4. TAs are responsible for keeping the LAN tidy.

5. When a class is using the LAN, the TA assists the teacher, demonstrating how software works, and even how a lesson might be enhanced by using some aspect of the LAN.

Basic Rules for the LAN

Post the rules so that everyone is aware that the computer lab is a working environment.

1. The purpose of the LAN is to provide students and teachers access to computers during the school day. *I will be in the LAN only when I have a legitimate need to use a computer.*

2. I will be responsible for the equipment in the LAN. *I will do nothing which will damage or deface the equipment and software in the LAN.*

3. Copyright laws exist to protect authors and their ideas. *I will not bring illegal software into the LAN. I will not use the LAN computers to illegally copy programs.*

4. *When I log-off the computer I will clean up and prepare my workstation for the next user.*

Basic Management Tips

1. Create a file-naming system everyone uses consistently. The filename might contain the student's initials and the date.

2. Create a start-up and shut-down routine everyone uses con-sistently. This routine should include procedures for logging-on, saving files in the correct folders, and logging-off.

I used the following procedures:

Logging-On

1. turn on computer

2. enter class name (e.g. Mon2 = Monroe, period 2)

3. press TAB key and type password

4. press RETURN key

5. double-click the file server and the application desired

It should be noted that because we have two file servers (i.e., Programs and Storage), students needed some initial guidance. The Programs file server was used to launch applications, and the Storage file server was used to save documents. It gets equally slippery if your workstations have hard disks, because students will unwittingly save files on the workstation hard disk until they learn how to navigate the network.

The only tricky part in saving files over a network is making sure students save their documents to the correct folders and not to the hard disks. We avoided problems by "write protecting" the hard disks (see the file server manual). Then, when a student saved a file, it could only be saved to the correct folder because the student only had access to that folder.

When students want to save to their own disk, all they have to do is insert their data disk in the workstation disk drive and select the correct drive before saving. Even though this is a relatively easy procedure, it may take students a few times to get familiar with where their work is going.

Logging-Off

1. Save your work.
2. Quit the program.
3. Shut down or restart the computer.
4. Clean up the area, and prepare the workstation for next user.

I review the above procedures and students copy them into their learning logs before we go to the computer lab.

The screens in Figure 21 show basic log-on procedures. The first screen shows what a student sees after the system disk is inserted and the computer is turned on. The student enters the class name and period number, moves the cursor to the password line, and enters the password. Dots show up instead of the password so a student's access remains confidential.

Although we use a Macintosh system, an IBM network operates similarly. Screens will look different, but students at my school use both an IBM Novell network and a Macintosh Appleshare network with equal ease.

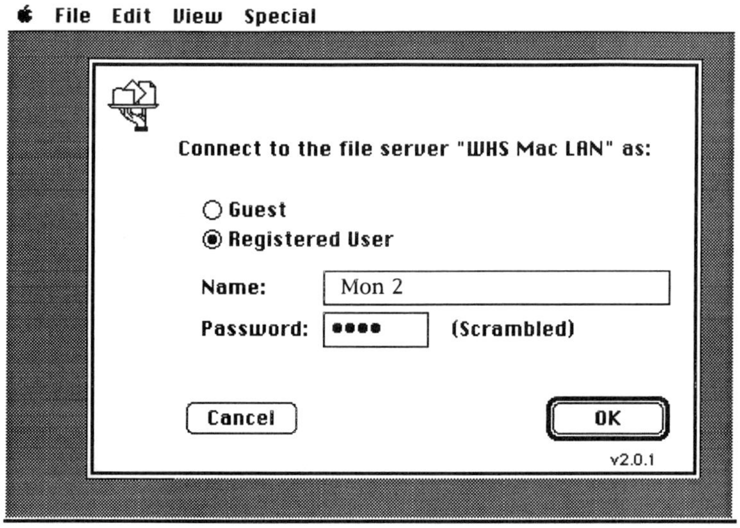

The screen below shows what the start-up screen looks like. Note the file-server icons. The following screen illustrates the next step. The Programs icon is darkened. The student has selected the icon by clicking twice on it.

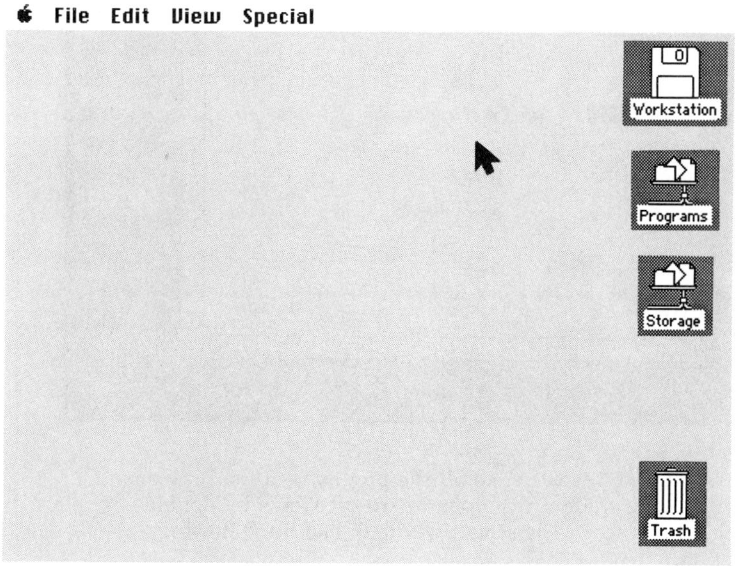

Figure 21. Log-on Screens.

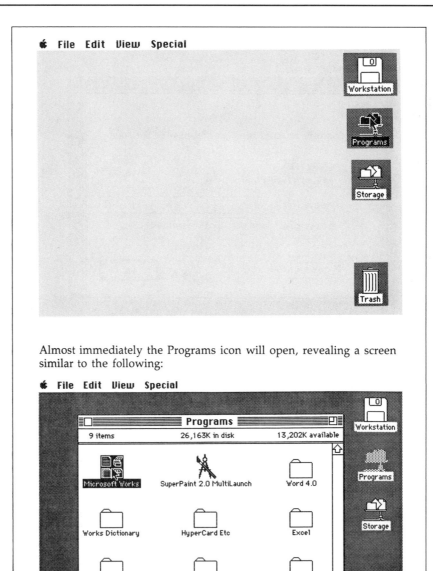

Almost immediately the Programs icon will open, revealing a screen similar to the following:

Now the student has access to all the programs in the Programs file. In this case, the student will open Microsoft Works by double-clicking on that icon. The screen will look like the following illustration.

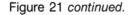

Figure 21 *continued.*

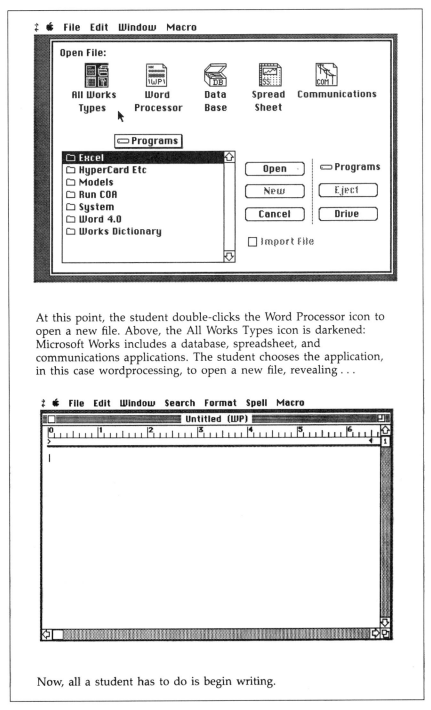

At this point, the student double-clicks the Word Processor icon to open a new file. Above, the All Works Types icon is darkened: Microsoft Works includes a database, spreadsheet, and communications applications. The student chooses the application, in this case wordprocessing, to open a new file, revealing . . .

Now, all a student has to do is begin writing.

Figure 21 *continued.*

Access Privileges and Sample Log-On Procedure

All networking software packages allow the LAN administrator to set access privileges. This is a simple procedure, and I will not explain it here. See your networking software administrator's handbook for clear and detailed explanations.

A warning is important here. I do not recommend setting up individual access privileges, because each individual must be given a password and access to applications and folders. If a problem occurs with the system, any passwords or access privileges not routinely backed up will be lost. The LAN administrator will then have to re-enter names and passwords and reset access privileges.

I avoid this potential problem by setting up class access privileges. For example, if you are a student in Monroe's second period class, you log-on by typing Mon2 (the user name) and then typing the password for that particular class. Only students in my second period class know the password.

Individual users who regularly use the lab are given accounts with individual passwords, but these users are responsible for backing up their files. Because TAs need access to everything on the LAN, they either log-on using their own names and a password chosen by them or they are allowed to use the administrator's user name and password. I handpick my Technical Assistants so they can be trusted. These students know they are responsible for maintaining the security of the network, and in three years, not one of them has tampered with files or abused their power.

The following screens in Figure 22 demonstrate what general users see after they log-on to the system. As the first screen illustrates, the user has opened both the Programs and the Storage file servers. Both have open and restricted folders. The white folders are open to general users, and the gray are not. The person who has logged-on in the example can open the Classes or RegUsers folders in the Storage file server, but will not have access to the folders unless he or she is a member of one of the groups.

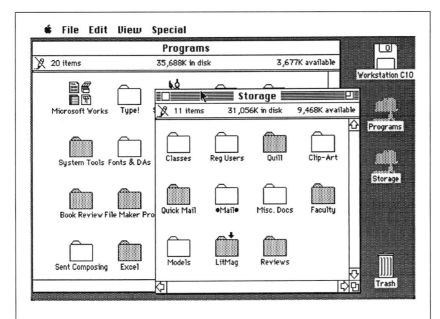

The first screen shows the folder LitMag with an arrow over it—it is a drop folder. The arrow means that anyone can drop a file into it, but will not be able to retrieve it later, exactly like a mailbox. Only those with passwords, in this case, students working on the magazine, can open and retrieve the files.

The following screen illustrates the opened Reg Users folder. Now, this student has access to only the white folders—DIEU and Public Domain.

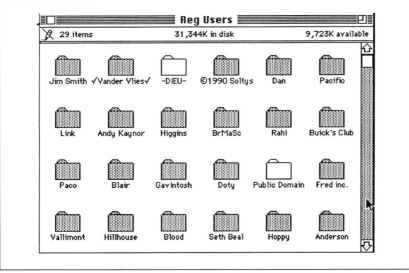

Figure 22. Additional Screens.

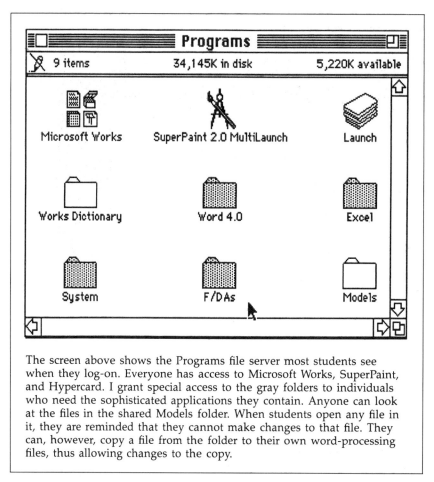

The screen above shows the Programs file server most students see when they log-on. Everyone has access to Microsoft Works, SuperPaint, and Hypercard. I grant special access to the gray folders to individuals who need the sophisticated applications they contain. Anyone can look at the files in the shared Models folder. When students open any file in it, they are reminded that they cannot make changes to that file. They can, however, copy a file from the folder to their own word-processing files, thus allowing changes to the copy.

Figure 22 *continued.*

I cannot emphasize enough the fact that the kind of hardware you choose to use is immaterial. An IBM network using Microsoft Windows looks similar to a Macintosh system. What *is* important is using the network to teach writing and thinking.

The principles for any network are the same. It is what students do and how teachers develop curriculum that matters. The tool should be transparent. It should be the means, and not an end in itself.

Planning for Success

Certainly, some thought should be given to goals, especially if you have to convince the school board, the community, and the principal that investing in a networked computer lab is important. My central premise is that writing and thinking with computers enriches learning in any discipline. In this section, I offer some thoughts you might want to adopt or at least consider before investing any money in a networked computer lab.

Why Invest in a Networked Computer Lab?

- To increase students' fluency (i.e., their ability to become articulate within the field of discourse characteristic of a subject).
- To become comfortable with and expert at asking productive questions about a subject.
- To formulate a coherent and probing understanding of several aspects of a subject.
- To become an explicator (and perhaps an advocate) to other audiences about certain aspects of a subject.
- To develop desired attitudes about a subject (e.g., curiosity, persistence, humility, enthusiasm).
- To seek and make connections between a subject and other subjects (e.g., English-math, history-art, and so forth).

To really explore innovative uses of technology, consider developing some collaborative projects with teachers in other disciplines. Such discussions will help clarify what kinds of changes in perspective are needed because collaborative planning takes a lot of time. If you feel energetic, read over the following prospectus and then ask a few colleagues from other disciplines to join you and your students in exploring writing, drawing, and calculating across the disciplines.

A Prospectus for a Networked Lab

Planning for the LAN requires a larger vision. Think about how writing, drawing, calculating, and thinking with computers might change your approach to your subject and your students. Think about how writing, drawing, calculating, and thinking with computers might change a student's attitude about the subject. Think about how teachers can collaborate with one another on projects.

1. Proposed Goals:
   - To think innovatively and collaboratively about how computer use can change students' level of understanding.
   - To plan specific teaching/learning strategies involving the LAN.

- To share LAN experiences consistently with other teachers and students.
- To evaluate students' and teachers' reactions to LAN use.

2. Proposed Lessons:

- Devise a plan that includes

    a. the instructional goal(s).

    b. the evaluation strategies.

    c. the assignments and activities (reading, writing, drawing, calculating, and other kinds of composing).

- When assigning lessons to be completed in the LAN, consider

    a. how an assignment supports an instructional goal (what students should eventually know or learn).

    b. what activities will insure success of the assignment.

    c. time constraints.

    d. the effect on students as they learn software and hardware (what basic information students need to begin the assignment).

3. Plan, Plan, Plan:

- Schedule meetings before the school year begins to

    a. consider various cross-curricular writing and thinking strategies.

    b. examine sample lessons by participating members as a basis for brainstorming ways of integrating the LAN into the curriculum to extend or enhance previously established instructional goals.

    c. begin working collaboratively in designing feasible LAN uses. These might include

        (1) access to information relevant to course (textbooks, library, specially created databases, images)

        (2) informal writing by students in response to teacher instructions, questions, self-generated reactions to course material

        (3) collaborative learning activities involving writing, calculating, manipulation of databases, spreadsheets, preparation of visual materials, and telecommunications

        (4) individual long-term projects involving writing, calculating, manipulation of databases, spreadsheets, preparation of visual materials, and telecommunications

■ As a team plan to meet twice monthly to continue planning together. (See chapter 4.)

Inservice

It is imperative that an inservice schedule be set up before teachers are expected to use technology with their students. Using technology in a subject takes time because the instructor must learn how it operates before attention can be turned to thinking about innovative ways to use it. It is generally agreed that, depending on the person, mastering a program requires between thirty and fifty hours. Teachers and especially administrators need to keep this in mind before they begin designing thoughtful learning situations that will challenge their students. As the school year progresses, more sophisticated features of a program can be incorporated into the lessons you are already using, adding texture and depth.

Although this is an obvious point, you might want to work through many of the lessons in this book so you can anticipate any potential problems as well as adapt them for your specific needs. Because none of us teach the same way or in the same situations, feel free to alter the lessons in this book.

Supplies

When setting up a local area network, you need to make sure you have at least 200 disks if your computer workstations do not have hard disks. If you expect students to save all their files on their own disks, then you will need as many disks as users. If you set up the LAN so students log-on and save their documents in class folders on a common hard disk, then 100–150 disks should be adequate. The smallest hard disk I would purchase for storing shared files would be 240 megabytes. Make sure you have adequate storage containers for all disks. It is a good idea to have a small flip-n-file for each workstation. These can be purchased at any office or discount supply store for under five dollars apiece. The LAN administrator will need additional flip-n-files and a secure closet to store all master copies of software. Stock plenty of white bonded paper and eight or nine laser cartridges. There is nothing more frustrating than running out of paper or laser cartridges. I also suggest purchasing a few extra phone-net connectors and mouse components, just in case a few are stolen. Finally, give some thought to where you want to house the main computer that acts as the file server for the lab. You might put it in an office or closet so it is readily accessible whenever new accounts need to be created but not available to everyone who enters the lab.

Introduction to Word Processing

This section is an inservice presentation I developed for teachers some time ago. It is designed as a primer for teachers anxious both about learning word processing themselves and about introducing the skill to their students. The first part of the presentation is meant to help teachers learn about word processing. The second part is a guide to help them teach word processing to their students. Because programs now come with interactive tutorials, the student lesson file in Figure 23 may now seem unnecessary.

If your school cannot afford computer workstations with hard disks, your students will have to boot-up the computer with the tutorial disk. When they finish, make sure all tutorial disks are returned and the original start-up disk is inserted in the disk drive for the next student who wants to log-on to the network. What all this means is that whoever is supervising the LAN will have to develop a simple disk management system. Otherwise, disks will surely disappear, and you and your colleagues will spend more time looking for lost or stolen disks than learning about the wonders of the word processor, the database, the spreadsheet, etc.

So, if your district cannot or will not purchase computers with hard disks, you may find having limited technology is only slightly better than having no technology.

Either way, you will still have to think about how you will introduce your students to the simplest application—word processing.

Getting Started with Word Processing

Step One

Find out where the computers are and go there.

Step Two

Ask someone about the manual that goes with the word-processing program you are using. Preview the manual, paying attention to only those parts of the program that which might be useful to you. If there are introductory disks or tutorials for the program, ask someone for assistance, and then sit down in front of a computer and run them.

Step Three

Find a partner and work together. Learning word processing is easy, because all you need to know is how to:

a. open the program

b. initialize or format a new disk

c. create a new file (New..)

d. open/retrieve a file

e. insert text

f. select and delete text

g. move the cursor or mouse

h. select and cut-and-paste text

i. print

j. save

k. save as/rename

l. quit

The program handbook will tell you how to do all of the above. Use it as a reference whenever you get stuck.

Step Four

Learn the specifics of the program with your partner. Set aside about three to four hours together, investing prep time to learn the program.

Tips:

a. invest your prep time

b. practice word processing by creating several assignments with it

c. play with the program, working through the activities in step three

Step Five

Before taking a class to the computer lab, make sure you

a. plan ahead, plan ahead, plan ahead

b. have students keep a computer procedures log

Step Six

At some time you will have to familiarize students with terminology. Both you and they should know and understand the following terms:

a. disk

b. cursor

c. delete

d. disk drive

e. keyboarding

f. save and save as

g. boot

h. open or load

i. file and filename

j. mouse

k. program/application

l. menu

m. scroll

Students can review the terminology, the start-up and shut-down procedures, and how to save files in the classroom. If you have a keyboarding program, make sure every student has a chance to develop simple proficiency with it. They can continue keyboarding practice well after the class has started using the computer.

Introducing Word Processing to Students: The First Five Sessions

Keep in mind that my students and I have done quite a bit of preparation and talking before we wander into the computer lab. Every student has notes about the basic procedures in their learning log. I pair students up so, as partners, they will work through the first few days together.

Day One

1. Ask the rest of the class to watch as you show one set of partners the start-up procedures and how to open the program.

2. If you have a PC viewer, have the entire class follow your procedures as you demonstrate them on the overhead.

3. Model opening the program while everyone watches.

4. Allow time for trouble-shooting. Someone always has problems and that's okay.

5. Request that students ask one another for help when a problem occurs.

6. Ask students to find in their learning logs the procedure for creating and saving a file. Have partners create a new file and begin writing. (It is a good idea to have several prompts ready for students who insist they haven't anything to say. For example, students might write about writing with a computer.)

7. Demand that your students write enough to fill up the screen without stopping to edit.

8. After the screen is full, let them mouse around. Have them practice moving the cursor, deleting text, inserting text, and changing text styles and fonts. (Remind them about highlighting text before making changes.)

9. Leave them alone and let students play with their words on the screen. (I wander around the LAN and act as a consultant when needed, but more important, I keep my mouth shut, forcing students to use their notes and each other.) Have students save their files using their initials and the date.

Day Two

1. Repeat start-up procedure, and tell students to wait for further instructions.

2. Demonstrate how to retrieve a file. Ask students to open the files they saved the last time. Give them a few minutes to play with the old files.

3. Ask students to open the "Lesson" file. (This can be tricky at first if you are on a network, because students will need practice navigating the system. In a stand-alone lab, students open the "Lesson" file the same way they did their own files.)

4. Whatever kind of system you have, make sure the procedures are routine.

5. Ask students to scroll through the "Lesson" file, reading it and noting its problems. (See Figure 23, page 80.)

6. Talk about the problems. Tell them their job is to correct the file and then rename and save it. Have students rename the file with their initials and the date.

7. Demonstrate how to cut-and-paste text before giving the class thirty minutes to complete the task. Again, demonstrations are easier with a PC viewer.

Your "Lesson" file might include the program options students will be using most. You might develop a series of lesson files that require students to use the spell checker, the find-and-replace option, or the page format options.

The "Lesson" file in Figure 23 was typed as is, saved, and used to help students learn how to use Microsoft Works. In a networked computer lab, lesson files can be powerful instructional tools.

Day Three

1. Repeat start-up procedure and open the "Lesson" file students corrected the day before. Review their corrections. Allow time for playing with the font, size, justification, style, and spacing options. Twenty minutes should be enough time to make them feel proficient with these options.

2. Ask students to return all the text to normal, showing them how to select all of the text. At the top of the file, ask students to write their name, the date, and the period. (They will have to insert two or three returns to create space for this.)

3. Demonstrate the Print Preview option. Ask students to double-check their file, using the Print Preview option before printing the corrected "Lesson" file.

Day Four

Repeat start-up procedure and open the file the students wrote on Day One. Give students twenty to thirty minutes to write you a letter about what they learned since Day One. The letter should include changes in fonts, type size, style, spacing, and justification. The letter should also include some speculation about how using the computer might help their writing.

Day Five

Real writing begins.

Additional considerations and strategies include:

1. Invisible writing with or without a partner (turning the monitor down)
2. Dialogue with an adjacent computer (switching keyboards)
3. Working with multiple files (windows)

As you read through this file, you should become familiar with some of the features of **Microsoft Works.** *Basically, this lesson is designed to help you. Read this file carefully and follow the instructions about the changes that obviously need to be made. Make sure you read the entire file first. Good Luck!*

When you are finished, you will need to save this file, but before you do, you need to make sure you don't save it over the original file. Here's how you rename this corrected version without disturbing the original. Using the mouse, move down the cursor to the File part of the menu at the top of my screen. Click once, holding it down so you can see all the options under the File Menu. Move the pointer down the menu until Save As . . . is black. Let up on the mouse button. You now see what is called a dialogue box. At the top center of the box is the name of the disk where the original lesson was opened. This is also where the file you are working on now will be saved. About halfway down the dialogue box are the words "Save Document As:" Please notice that the original lesson is now in black. Type your initials and today's date. Did you notice that the original file name was replaced by what you just typed? Now click once on the save button. You have just renamed and saved this file. The original, with all its mistakes, is still on the disk.

Now, what want you to do is read this paragraph. Someofthewordsarejammed together and Iwantyoutoseparate them. All you have to do is move the cursor to the point where you want to insert a space and click once, then press the space bar once to insert a space btween the words. Repeat this procedure until all the words jammed together in this paragraph are separated. Oops! I made a mistake on the line above. Did you see I misspelled "between"? Would you please insert an **e** between the **b** and the **t** in "btween" in this paragraph. Thanks. Before you go on to the next paragraph, I want you to delete all the text beginning with "Oops!" and ending with "Thanks." The way to delete a block of text is simple. Move the cursor to the beginning of the text and then

---

Figure 23. Sample Lesson File. *Note to Teacher:* I inserted extra spaces between paragraphs to make cutting and pasting easier. Beginners often select too much, including returns, and that can cause a mess and a lot of frustration.

4. Merging files (templates or electronic response groups)

5. Cooperative work takes time

6. Redesigning lessons to take advantage of technology also takes time

Teaching writing and thinking with computers, whether in a local area network or with stand-alone computers, has both advantages and disadvantages.

Disadvantages

1. Sharing is time-consuming.

2. Assignments take longer to complete.

3. Pre-planning and cooperation are vital within the class and the school.

4. Keyboarding deficiencies can cause student frustration with word processing.

5. Beware of product preoccupation. All writing produced on a computer looks professional.

---

click the mouse button and hold it down. Don't let up on the button. Drag the cursor over the text you want to delete. Notice that the text is in black. This is called **highlighting.** Make sure you have highlighted the text you want to delete and then press the backspace key once. Delete that text now and go to the next paragraph.

Before you save this file, I would like you to do some writing. Add about three lines of text here, filling out this paragraph. Make sure you don't press the return key unless you want to start a new paragraph. Make sure this paragraph is the second to last one.

You probably noticed that the paragraphs in this file are not in the correct order. What I would like you to do **first** is reorganize the paragraphs in this file. Follow these procedures: move the cursor to the beginning of the paragraph you want to move (Cut and Paste). Click the mouse button once, and, while holding the button down, drag the cursor over all the text in the paragraph you want to move. All the text you want to move is now highlighted. Now, move the cursor to the Edit Menu. Click and hold until you see the word Cut. Drag the cursor down and highlight Cut. The text you highlighted in the document is now gone. It isn't really gone, of course. Anyway, now move the cursor to where you want the text to be inserted. Click the mouse button once. The cursor should now be blinking at the spot where you want the text to be inserted. Now prepare yourself for a wonderful bit of Mac magic. Move the mouse to the Edit Menu again and select the word Paste. Voila! All the text you highlighted is now inserted. Now your job is to put all these paragraphs in the correct order. Oh yeah, if you think you know how to cut and paste, you can delete this entire paragraph.

Figure 23 *continued.*

Advantages

1. Sharing provides built-in consultants.

2. Students stay with one piece longer so the teacher can conference during the writing.

3. The necessity of pre-planning often brings departments together.

4. Students' and teachers' attitudes change:

    a. teacher as consultant during the writing process;

    b. student as participant in education;

    c. revision isn't tedious.

5. Students will find ways to present their ideas.

6. Teachers can extend requirements, focusing on thinking and not just form.

3 Extending the Uses of Technology

This chapter chronicles how St. Joseph's School grew with the technology to help students think through problems. I think you will see that a little imagination will take you as far (perhaps farther) as the latest, greatest, space-age technology. I like what the staff at St. Joseph's has done, because their work truly reflects the spirit of this book—that you don't have to have much to do a lot. While Kathy Marion and I wrote this chapter, we also spent some time imagining the fourth Camp Tech.

Imagining and Making the Future

It was January, a typical dreary, chilly, day in Seattle when the junior high department at St. Joseph's School sat around the faculty lunchroom, brainstorming unique ways they might use computers. They had already spent several months talking and thinking about their computer curriculum, when Jim Leers quipped, "Why don't we develop a camp. We could call it Camp Tech." They must have been ripe for the idea because the junior high staff embraced it immediately. Little did they know the amount of time, energy, and plain hard work that would be needed to pull this off for 180 junior high students and six staff members. Even though that first Camp Tech experience drained them, they have recently finished their fourth Camp Tech.

Camp Tech I

These teachers agreed to set aside a full week in April for the camp. Students were assigned to cabins, and teachers took on the role of cabin counselors. On the first day of "camp," students arrived wearing shorts and carrying sack lunches. They were directed to the registration table where they received their cabin assignments. This was camp, and each teacher/counselor extended the scenario by wearing a teacher-designed Camp Tech cap and T-shirt. The outfit was completed by an essential camp tool, the whistle.

Although the normal class day was suspended, normal subjects were not. The junior high staff took on the responsibility of developing a plan for

A radically condensed version of this chapter appears in *Momentum*, February 1992.

the curriculum in their respective content areas, a plan that incorporated group work and computers. For example, the language arts teachers decided each cabin would write and publish a student handbook for the school. In contrast, the science/physical education teachers used a spreadsheet to calculate physical fitness test results to see which cabin was the most fit. During the initial planning, the teachers selected software that was easy to learn. They didn't want to burden themselves or their students, so the junior high teachers decided to stick with the applications they were already using—AppleWorks and LOGO.

The junior high staff have survived four Camp Techs, each one evolving into something more elaborate than the one previous. Primarily, however, the goal is to create, in a camp-like atmosphere, a situation that requires the implementation of technology to solve a problem. After that first Camp Tech, two lasting principles emerged:

1. technology is more than computers
2. problem-solving isn't dependent on arbitrary subject divisions

For example, a technology expert from a local educational service district visited Camp Tech. This expert gave mini-lessons on computer literacy and provided demonstrations that used technologies such as CD-ROM. Even though the students did not own such sophisticated systems, they learned about many ways in which technology can be integrated into education. Although rudimentary, these demonstrations gave students and teachers an inkling of how technology could be used to solve problems, think critically, and gather and synthesize information to insure flexibility, cooperation, tolerance, consensus, analysis, and communication.

There is too much information regarding the mechanics of setting up and operating Camp Tech to include here. The lessons students and teachers learned and the materials they developed could fill several volumes. (See the end of this chapter for a breakdown of hardware/software used for each Camp Tech.) That first Camp Tech and its successors pulled the junior high staff at St. Joseph's through those dark winter months and has energized their computer curriculum.

Camp Tech II

The following year, Kathy Marion and Mary Sifferman attended the National Conference on Computers in Education in Spokane, Washington. From that conference, Mary got a copy of a database called Power of the Nation States. To entertain themselves on the six-hour drive home, Kathy and Mary started brainstorming how it could be used with history classes. By the time they hit the Seattle city limits, Camp Tech II was solidified.

Camp Tech II would introduce students to the experience of power and powerlessness. Again, when the seventh and eighth graders registered for camp, they were assigned to "cabins," each one representing a global region. The students were informed that they would be playing an adapted version of Risk, a board game where players seek power and world domination. The junior high staff hoped that students would come to see how power affects their ability to participate in world events.

On that first day, cabins were given the task of creating a sub-database that included military, economic, and human resources. After studying a map of the world, cabins were also required to divide existing countries into regions. Students accomplished this by studying, selecting, and matching records provided in the enormous and complex Power of the Nation States database. The cabin that completed the task of subdividing the countries into six regions (one per cabin) and then creating six sub-databases for each region first got to select the region they wanted to represent.

Weeks before Camp Tech II began, the history teacher had had the students discuss what they thought made a country powerful. Based on what students generated, teachers knew which categories of Power of the Nation States students would be using when the scenario began.

Once a cabin knew which region it represented, it then established an identity. Each cabin (i.e., region) used Print Shop to create its own flag and to develop a world map that depicted the military power of all regions. To enrich the scenario, cabins composed a national anthem and selected an Olympic team. Simultaneously, ambassadors and diplomats were elected and began negotiations with the other regions, establishing alliances that insured their security while improving their global status. To reinforce written communication, no oral diplomacy was allowed. Students acting as ambassadors wrote international communiqués on their computers and then "mailed" them in a diplomatic pouch (i.e., disk), trying to convince other regions to help them acquire those resources they lacked. For example, regions lacking economic strength forged partnerships with richer regions. The overall goal, of course, was to see if students could maintain the delicate balance between power and peace. In doing so, they had to clearly write down and communicate their region's position, hoping they had articulated the benefits of peace and the consequences of aggression.

Throughout the week, students used computers exclusively to continually update their and the other regions' power bases. Every day, after a Risk-War session, regions used the database and spreadsheet of AppleWorks to accurately reflect the day's events, graphing their region's distribution of military, economic, and human resources.

On the third day, dismayed students watched their world collapse as regions maneuvered for power instead of harmony. Regions demanded a United Nations conference to help mend differences. This demand caught the staff by surprise, because the United Nations Assembly was not part of the original scenario. But students needed a safe place where diplomats could speak freely, without retribution, about issues concerning their region and the world. Instinctively, they understood that world war seemed inevitable. Perhaps what precipitated this action was that the Camp Tech scenario had seeped into these students' daily lives. Students who normally ate lunch together and played soccer at recess were now enemies. Students were not able to "turn off" the game. The issues in the game touched a deeper level, sounded a stronger chord in them, and somehow they knew a balance, a truce, had to be reached before friendships were destroyed. Who would have thought a game could have caused such internal chaos and external anger?

During that mock U. N. General Assembly questions flew and debates raged as diplomats and ambassadors read prepared statements representing a region's position on war. Some felt other regions should not be allowed to participate in the planned Olympics because they were too militaristic. Ambassadors wanted to boycott aggressive regions that had violated the ethics of the Olympics when they invaded weaker regions. Amid chants such as "EASEA, out of Africa," the U. N. General Assembly eventually voted that all regions could participate in the Olympics. All of this was reminiscent of the real nations who withdrew from the 1980 Olympics when the Soviet Union invaded Afghanistan.

World war was averted, and the next day students held the opening ceremonies of the Olympics. Each nation, dressed in its colors and carrying its computer-generated flag, marched into the "Olympic Arena." Bearing the Olympic eternal flame, a representative from each region ran one lap around the track. The host region representative was the last runner, and just like the real thing, ran up a flight of stairs and lit the Olympic torch. The president of the host region gave the opening remarks and ended with, "Let the games begin."

The competition produced by the Olympics and the unequal distribution of power among the nations helped to intensify world tensions. This led to a strong desire for peace by the end of Camp Tech II. All regions analyzed their positions of power and returned to the computer to revise peace plans their ambassadors could submit to the United Nations. The peace plans were read by a panel of teachers from the primary department. They selected the peace proposal that seemed to reflect the thoughts and desires of Seattle's retired Archbishop Hunthausen.

Unfortunately, some cabins could not overlook regional interests. Alliances based on power were so tempting that these regions were unable to abide by the peace plan. Much like the world today, students made plans, failed to enact them, and fell back on developing policies that encouraged the build-up of weapons. Students rationalized that a stockpile of weapons would keep the peace until an equitable distribution of power could bring about disarmament.

It was amazing to see how even these young minds had tacitly accepted a cold war mentality for solving global problems. Even so, the week concluded with a prayer service for peace and the presentation of the Hunthausen Humanitarian Award. This award was given to the region that did the most to foster peace in the world. Public school teachers might need to plan an end to hostilities more secular in nature.

Afterward, students reflected on their experiences. As you can see from the following comments, students were insightful:

- "It made me realize that war is mostly pride."
- "During the week, I paid more attention to the news and found that much we were experiencing in Camp Tech was really happening in the real world."
- "It helped us to experience negotiating and working with other people to resolve problems."
- "I learned more this week than I have learned in my whole life about making peace and the results of war."

Camp Tech III

Like the first Camp Tech, Camp Tech III started during a brainstorming session. Jim Leers shared his experience of participating in a videotaped commercial to sell a child's theater booster chair an inventor friend of his was marketing. Jim acted in the promotional tape and cracked up the junior high staff with his stories about his short-lived video career. As in the popular Andy Hardy movies where Mickey Rooney and Judy Garland brainstormed ways to make money ("Let's put on a show!"), the teachers began imagining Camp Tech III:

- "We could make a product and sell it."
- "We'll need a company."
- "The cabins could be corporations."
- "We could bring in consultants from the community."
- "Hey, I know someone, who . . . ."

By now, students knew something special happened on the junior high floor every spring. As they had for the previous Camp Techs, students registered and were assigned cabins. This year, however, when students registered, they were assigned a cabin color instead of a cabin name. It was crucial for students to establish their own corporate identity by developing that corporation's name, logo, jingle, and letterhead.

Students were informed that their cabins were mini-corporations and that their goal was to create a product that would be sold to our school's sixth graders. Students spent the first day setting up their corporations. Cabins selected a chief executive officer and managers in the following areas: advertisement, media, and product development. Each manager was responsible for making sure a department did its job and reported to the C.E.O. Responsibilities were as varied as the tasks. For example, the C.E.O. ran corporate meetings, coordinated the department efforts, and used Microsoft Works to manage the budget. The advertisement manager supervised the creation of billboards, newspaper and magazine ads, and direct mailings (i.e., junk mail). The ad department used SuperPaint, Studio One, Print Shop, WriteNow 2.2, Correct Grammar, Microsoft Works 2.0, Hypercard, and Hypercard Gallery to create newspaper and magazine ads. This department also used the mail-merge function of Works to send direct mail to the sixth grade. The media department developed a videotaped commercial for the corporation's product that would later be aired in the sixth-grade classes. This department also used VCR Companion, a product that superimposes text on the screen. The product development department designed and built the prototype and final product, including its packaging. To insure a profit, each department had to work cooperatively for the good of the corporation.

Students filled out job applications and wrote résumés for the positions they wanted. To make sure qualified candidates were selected fairly for specific jobs, the applications were read by teachers outside the junior high department. The application was designed with Microsoft Works. Students serious about landing the job of their choice polished their résumés on the computer. On the second day, job placements were announced in each cabin (i.e., corporation). It should also be noted that throughout the week, students dressed both for the scenario and for camp. Attire for the week included shirt and tie and shorts.

This scenario was richer than past Camp Techs, primarily because experts from the community and corporations were invited to participate. They came to consult with students as they developed their respective products. Guest speakers included inventors, a C.E.O., a graphic artist/designer, a drafter, a University of Washington engineering student, a patent lawyer, and a music specialist.

Once again, listen to what students had to say about the experience:

■ "It takes time to design, from the first prototype to the final product, and market a product."

■ "For eighth graders, I think we did a hell of a job. (P.S. that was the only way I could express myself.)"

■ "I learned that in picture ads, it should be bright and neat or very messy to catch someone's eye."

■ "I could have worked all the time but I would have died from stress."

■ "Our corporation used time very well, learning, being confused, figuring things out, and making things."

Obviously, these young entrepreneurs learned much about the corporate world. The last day of Camp Tech III was spent presenting products (at a Trade Fair) to sixth graders. Products were judged to be successful if they sold well. Students came to understand that it takes a team effort to conceive, design, and create a product. They learned quite a bit about marketing and how to adopt its strategies to increase consumerism. More important, they learned to work cooperatively in a venture that extended beyond themselves.

Camp Tech IV

The scenario for Camp Tech IV was called "Step into a Novel." Each cabin adopted the story of a novel, and in an effort to use technology to make meaning, developed activities that allowed students to step into their books.

The *Day No Pigs Would Die* cabin used Prodigy to locate recipes for creating a simple Shaker meal. The *Animal Farm* cabin scripted and video-taped a "TV Talk Show." The *Pigman* cabin expanded its learning walls, using a modem to interact with other schools through the AT&T Learning Network, inviting members from their AT&T Learning Circle on their Camp Tech adventure. The *Sex Education* cabin developed a curriculum for their book and submitted it to the author. She replied, praising their work.

In addition, Kathy Marion's *Pigman* cabin of seventh- and eighth-grade students corresponded with my high school students. Both groups read the same book and shared insights both believed were important. For example, students from St. Joseph's developed a diary that revealed important and secret information about the protagonist of the novel, and my students pretended to be three other characters who discovered this diary.

What did the campers have to say about this scenario?

■ From the *Wrinkle in Time* cabin: "I liked doing the 'eye collage' because it was fun looking for eyes and I liked the results. It was connected to the book because Charles Wallace was under a spell and Meg could tell by looking at his eyes."

- From the *Sex Education* cabin: "I liked how we practiced our religion by gathering clothing for a shelter for battered women and their children."

- From the *Flowers for Algernon* cabin: "The field trips helped me realize how hard it is for a person who has a disability to live."

An elaborate set-up is not necessary to establish a Camp Tech, but as indicated here, there tends to be a natural increase in sophistication. With each year, St. Joseph's Camp Tech has become more complex. The essential component is a dedicated staff willing to develop and execute a plan as a team. The junior high staff at St. Joseph's School made their Camp Tech scenarios work with the hardware and software available to them. Their primary goal continues to be to seek ways to create, in a camp-like atmosphere, a situation that requires the implementation of technology to solve problems.

Hardware and Software Required for Each Camp Tech

With each passing year, Camp Tech has become more elaborate as indicated by the kinds of hardware and software listed below. What is essential to the success of such a program is a willingness to patiently develop uses for technology that grow with the students and teachers.

Camp Tech I

3 Apple IIe computers in each cabin
1 Apple IIGS computer in each cabin
2 Apple IIe computers on a cart
AppleWorks software
LOGO software

Camp Tech II

3 Apple IIe computers in each cabin
2 Apple IIGS computers in each cabin
6 Apple IIGS computers in the hall
  serving as diplomatic workstations
AppleWorks software
Print Shop graphics program
Power of the Nation States database

Camp Tech III

7 Macintosh Plus computers with
  20–MB hard drives
8 Apple IIGS computers
2 VCRs with televisions
2 Camcorders
Microsoft Works 2.0 software
WriteNow 2.2 software
Correct Grammar software
SuperPaint painting program
Hypercard hypertext program

Camp Tech IV

7 Macintosh Plus computers with
  20–MB hard drives
8 Apple IIGS computers
2 VCRs with televisions
2 Camcorders
Microsoft Works 2.0 software
WriteNow 2.2 software
Correct Grammar software
SuperPaint painting program
Hypercard hypertext program

Hypercard Gallery hypertext program
Studio One
VCR Companion
Print Shop graphics program

Hypercard Gallery hypertext program
Studio One
VCR Companion
Print Shop graphics program
2400 baud modem and dedicated phone line for communicating with other schools or classes

If you would like more information about how to establish your own Camp Tech, please write Kathy Marion, St. Joseph's School, 700 18th Ave. East, Seattle, Washington 98112.

Publishing Student Work Using Desktop Publishing

Publishing student work via a local area network is easier than with a stand-alone computer lab, because networking software allows the LAN administrator to establish drop folders—folders that act like post office boxes. (See Access Privileges and Sample Log-On Procedures.) Students can put a file into such a folder, mailing it, but they cannot take files out. Only the group or individual who has been given access to the drop folder can retrieve these files. The beauty of creating a drop folder is that the contributed writing or artwork doesn't have to be re-typed or re-created by the person who collects and lays out prospective works for publication.

I like to include students as much as I can in publishing activities, but I take a hands-off attitude. When we are developing the literary arts magazine or a class anthology, I ask for one or two volunteers willing to read the submissions in the drop folder and lay them out. Selecting the best submissions is not an issue if you are creating a class newsletter or anthology, because every student should be included in such publications.

Even if you do not have a powerful desktop publishing program such as Pagemaker, most word-processing programs allow a user to create linked columns and to import graphics. One of the reasons I am so keen on Microsoft Works is that the word-processing part of this software allows users to import and manipulate graphics easily. Setting up linked columns with Works is also easy, and student editors can create a template complete with decorative header and footer with very little fuss. (A template is a standard page layout into which text and graphics may be placed.)

Of course, creating a class newsletter or anthology is possible with scissors, paste, and a photocopy machine, but it creates a huge mess and takes extra time. This is probably why most teachers do not want to bother with such activities.

In contrast, using computers and a desktop publishing program to create such publications requires much less mess and effort. Once the student editors lay out the class newsletter or anthology, all I need to do is have it duplicated and either stapled or bound. Duplication is simple and so is binding. The easiest way to bind an anthology is to staple it three times along the left edge and then use book tape to bind it. As always, my student editors collect the collated and duplicated publication and then staple and bind it. The result is a handsome and homemade book. Most photocopy machines can handle forty-pound cover stock, so creating a front and back for the anthology is equally easy. KISS (keep it simple, stupid) is my motto, and our school's networked computer lab has certainly helped me in this respect.

I have created several Pagemaker and Microsoft Works templates modeled after current magazine layouts and placed them in a shared folder. Students can either use one of these templates for their work or design their own magazine layout. I don't have time to teach my students a great deal about desktop publishing; programs such as Pagemaker are complex. But I do try to at least get them started. The professional models provide an important kind of framework. Figure 24 shows three sample shared magazine layouts.

Figure 24. Sample Screens of Magazine Layout.

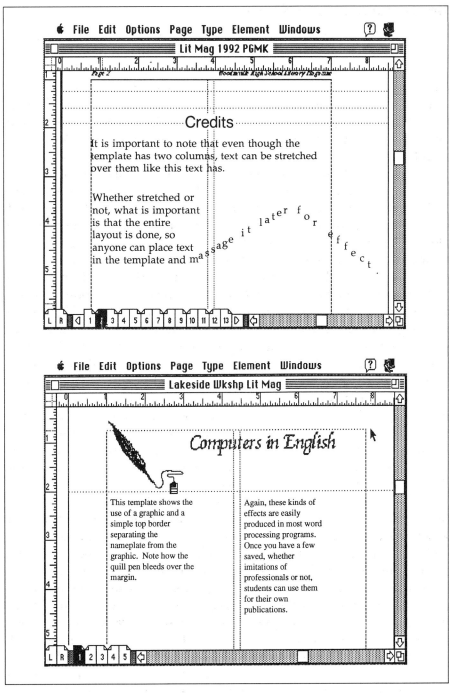

Figure 24 *continued.*

Telecommunications: A Primer

No doubt you have heard and read quite a bit about telecommunications and distance learning and have written them off because it all sounds beyond you. Actually, telecommunications doesn't require down dishes and satellite link-ups, or even a NASA mentality. Basically, all you need is a phone line, a computer, and a modem. In fact, if you have about $100.00, you can purchase a combination FAX/modem and then link your computer to your existing telephone. Voilà, you are linked to the world.

A word of caution is needed here. Because most of us do not even have the time to read the periodicals we subscribe to, it is foolish and maybe even dangerous to think we might, as William Wresch (1984) says, "surf the tidal wave of information" generated by the global electronic community. Our first concern is having access to information. The problem afterward is knowing what to do with it once we have it. As with most important human endeavors, it is how we transform information that determines privilege and power. It's a humbling and frustrating experience to tap into a CD-ROM database or a large database such as InterNet. Like a shopper given carte blanche in a department store, it's difficult to know where to start. A cursory look at the U.S. Atlas CD-ROM database, or any large bank of information, whether online or in print, will drive even the most enthusiastic shopper out of the mall. The user as consumer doesn't work very well for telecommunications. Most assumptions about how we live our lives are rarely tested until we are teetering at the edge of a canyon. Such issues as the explosion of information, who has access to such information, and how this power should or should not be used find us at the brink of such an abyss.

It seems to me that we have several choices. We could act as if the world isn't being transformed, as if new information is not being generated every second; or we might take a deep breath, accept our fallibility, and get on with making intelligent decisions about what we should attend to and why. It is clear to me that I want access to information so that I can transform it, personalizing those sterile figures so they support and clarify my message. And because I can recast raw data as bar charts, line graphs, and pie charts, because the computer allows me to transform information, helping me reshape it, I can be an agent for change instead of a slave to it. The issue is using banks of information and computers and software to solve problems and make connections. What matters is building bridges between people.

Let me backtrack a little. The simplest way to think about telecommunications is that it is any exchange of information over time or distance. Although most references to telecommunications involve a computer connected to a modem by a telephone line, a simple local area network that allows file sharing or the ability to send messages through electronic mail are also forms of telecommunication. And so is being connected to a CD-ROM database. You don't need a satellite dish and a microwave antenna to join the telecommunications forum.

If you want to gain access to dynamic databases or bulletin boards, you will need a personal computer, a modem or FAX/modem, a telephone line, and communications software. If you use Microsoft Works, you will find that it comes with communications software. Then all that's required is to find someone to join you in a conversation. And there are a lot of places to begin. What I would initially advise you to do is talk with other teachers in your district and find out if anyone is willing to set up an exchange. I suggest keeping it simple at first: ask students to talk about questions or concerns related to literature, or ask them to send poems, stories, or essays back and forth as a kind of long-distance writing group. Be assured that starting small will give you time to get comfortable with telecommunications and give you and your students time to imagine what to do next.

Of course, once you let students know you have a modem, you'll be swamped with requests to use it and inundated with bulletin board phone numbers students will insist do everything from expand their personal horizons to link the school to the world. Believe half of what your students tell you, but, instead of getting cranky, sit down with your most enthusiastic bulletin board (BBS) users and look at what local bulletin boards have to offer. In the Seattle area, a local teacher has set up a bulletin board that acts as a kind of homework hotline. Students and teachers can join ongoing conversations about politics or AIDS; they can exchange opinions and say what's on their minds, primarily sharing concerns and ideas about the world. Students and teachers alike need to know they are not alone. Tapping into a bulletin board that has a specific subject orientation, such as education, diminishes alienation and increases communion—let's face it, understanding ourselves and others requires communication. It cannot be done alone.

Once you are confident, you might look to other telecommunication outlets such as Prodigy, AT&T Easy Link Services Learning Network, Iris Online Network, or BreadNET/ITC. You've probably seen the commercials about Prodigy and might be a bit wary of bringing it into your classroom. With a little imagination, however, Prodigy has innumerable uses. Basically it's a database, a huge storehouse of information. What you and your students do with that information will determine if the $15.00–$20.00 monthly charge is worth the price.

The AT&T Easy Link Service Learning Network costs about $300.00 a year and caters to schools. The Learning Network creates what it calls Learning Circles—a kind of electronic classroom. A Learning Circle generally lasts about ten weeks, and participating schools receive curricular materials and software. During the ten weeks, schools are allowed to make unlimited phone calls. The Learning Network puts students and teachers who have chosen the same issue (e.g., the environment, energy, travel, etc.) in touch with one another. Generally, a Learning Circle is limited to eight or ten classrooms. Through curricular materials and an online newsletter, participants explore and share an issue all the participants have negotiated.

The Iris Online Network is cheaper, but it is an open system. That means curricular materials are not provided, and the participants are not limited to small groups who are interested in similar issues. Iris is truly a multi-voiced bulletin board. When you log-on, you make selections as to what room (i.e., topic/subject/issue) you want to enter. Before you know it, you are immersed in an ongoing conversation. I suggest waiting until you are well versed in telecommunications etiquette and navigation before you attempt the Iris Online Network. Your wallet and ego will thank you.

The International Telecomputing Consortium (ITC) is associated with the Bread Loaf School of English network. BreadNET/ITC is a nonprofit bulletin board that links different teacher networks for collaborative projects or conferences. ITC is so new that standards and schedules have not yet been established, but generally a project lasts about seven weeks. ITC is a large bulletin board (like Iris), so you might want to practice using your modem and navigating around local bulletin boards with friends before taking a swim in an international stream.

The most promising telecommunication service is K–12 NET. K–12 NET is a loose collaboration of bulletin board systems that provides free teleconnectivity for teachers and students from kindergarten to twelfth grade. K–12 NET provides exchanges in curriculum areas, offers classroom projects like the AT&T Learning Network, and includes educational files obtained from NASA, the U.S. Department of Education, ERIC, and the American Library Association. K–12 NET also offers international connections to bulletin boards from Australia, England, Austria, Switzerland, Germany, Canada, Estonia, Russia, and other foreign countries. All these services can be offered because mail and files are uploaded and downloaded from one local bulletin board to the next. For example, if I want to send a message to my brother in Portland, Oregon, I use my modem and connect to a Seattle bulletin board that relays the message from one local board to the next until it reaches Portland. And the cost? Nothing.

The English Classroom in the Computer Age: Thirty Lesson Plans (Wresch, 1990) is a good book to consult if you are considering getting involved in telecommunications, because the first three lessons of section three provide some fine guidance about how to get started.

The following contacts should help get you started if you are interested in more specific information about particular networks.

AT&T Easy Link Services Learning Network
400 Interpace
Parsippany, New Jersey 07054
1-800-367-7225

Iris Online Network
P.O. Box 29429
Richmond, Virginia 23229
Voice mail: 202-298-0969   FAX: 703-841-9798

BreadNET/ITC
1250 24th St. NW
Suite 300
Washington, DC 20037
202-466-0533 (contact: Bill Wright)

K–12 NET
Check user group listings for your area.
For Seattle the K–12 NET BBS is:
Sea/Mac
206-725-6629 (this number can only be used if you have a modem)

Book Reviews with FileMaker Pro

One of the reasons I like using an application-based networked computer lab is that my students and I can dream up and share new uses for programs. All a software developer cares about is that you use the product and encourage others to do the same. Software companies like it when users dream up new and fun uses for their software that the developer hadn't imagined. This is especially true for the kinds of applications I purchase. Microsoft, Claris, and Aldus are all companies that design and produce software specifically for business. What these companies really do is create programs that give people authority over their work. The teachers I admire do exactly that: they give their students the tools they need to make sense of their world and their lives.

Not long ago, and it happens all the time, a student asked me if I could recommend a book. As usual, I hedged a bit, asked what the student liked reading, hoped I had some experience in the genre, and then suggested seeing the librarian. Every year students ask me about good books and fun books. Telling them about good books is easy—I tell students what colleges hope they will read. But I was always stumped when they asked about fun books, because, frankly, what I enjoy reading for fun didn't seem to amuse or work for many of the teenagers I taught. That's when I thought about using a business program to develop a database of student-generated book reviews.

I decided to use FileMaker Pro to develop a database called Book Review. Students are encouraged to write reviews of materials they are reading for fun. Students get credit for doing the book reviews, but I tell them that I don't want to read the reviews or grade them. These book reviews are not for me. They are for the students' peers. If you think students won't read for fun unless assigned to do so, then I recommend requiring students to do some optional reading over a quarter or trimester. Instead of writing, drawing, or giving oral reports about these readings, ask students to write a review for their peers. Tell them that the reviews will be published.

Think of Book Review as a way of giving students credit for fun reading, as a vehicle where they encourage each other to read. For example, you might expect students to write one book review for the quarter, pointing out to them that the review will be checked but not read by you.

Using Book Review

Let me show you what I have done. After a student logs-on to the network, he or she goes to the folder called Book Review, opens it, and then opens the file. The Book Review database is opened and the student sees the screen in Figure 25.

To create a new review, the student clicks the new review circle and a blank book review appears. All the student has to do is enter the required information. The same holds for any of the other four choices shown in Figure 25. When the student clicks on a particular circle, FileMaker Pro executes the command linked to it. This is an easy process. It took me about two hours to develop the database. It would have taken me less time, but I had never used the program before.

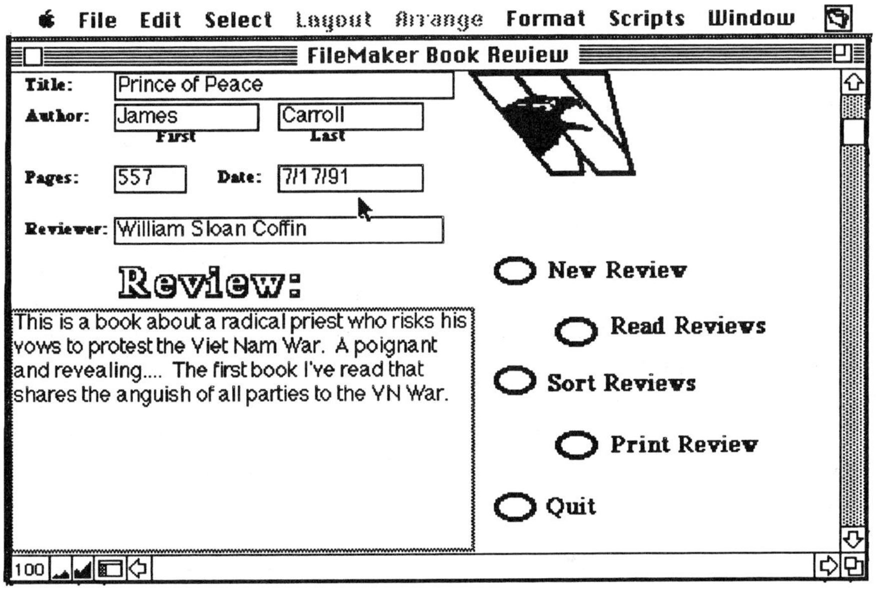

Figure 25. FileMaker Book Review.

After I developed Book Review, I put the database on the network in a folder anyone could access. Now our entire school has a student-maintained annotated bibliography of fun reading. And when we eventually get networked with other schools, we can begin building a district, state, or regional bibliographic database.

What I have described here is not particularly innovative, but it is one good way to show students that they too make useful contributions to the curriculum. When students ask me for a title of a good book, I enjoy referring them to what other students are reading. And because Book Review was created with a powerful database, a student can sort through the records in a variety of ways. For example, students can search by author, title, number of pages, and date; or, they can flip through the database much like they might thumb through a catalog. More important, the Book Review database is dynamic; new entries can be added at any time. And if a book is reviewed more than once, students can then compare these reviews and see how more than one reader reacted.

Student-generated databases are powerful tools for learning. It doesn't take much imagination to realize how history, biology, chemistry, or world-language teachers could use a database as an ongoing storehouse of knowledge for their disciplines. Over several years, students and teachers could develop a large and useful database.

Tracking Independent Reading

Like many of my other thoughtful lessons, this one came from Joan Fiset. It was designed to help students trace their interaction with a text. After students selected a book they wanted to read, and after they had a week to interact with their chosen text, students responded to the guided writings in their learning logs.

I gave my students the handout in Figure 26 after they chose a novel they wanted to read for fun. I asked them to respond to any two of the prompts in their learning logs as they read each week. I found students had more to say about what they were reading because of this exercise. Therefore, when they wrote their book reviews in the LAN, their responses were much more thoughtful.

Independent Reading Responses

During the next three weeks, instead of doing two speculative starters a week, I would like you to respond in your learning logs to any one of the following prompts each week. Be prepared to either read your response to your writing group or the entire class on a day to be designated later. I will check to see you have completed one of these Monday. Please have your learning log ready.

1. As you think ahead to your next day's reading, what possible direction might the story take? How do you hope the story will unfold?

2. What surprised you about what you've read so far? How does this change affect what might happen next in the story?

3. What feelings did you experience in response to events or characters (e.g., irritation, wonder, disbelief, recognition, dislike), and why do you think you responded that way?

4. What questions do you hope to have answered next by the story?

5. What startling or unusual words, phrases, expressions, or images did you come across in your reading that you would like to have explained or clarified? Which ones would you like to use in your own writing?

6. If the setting and characters were changed to reflect your own neighborhood and friends and acquaintances, how would the events of the story develop and why would that be so?

7. Have you ever had a dream or daydream that seemed similar to an event in this book? Try to describe the dream or daydream and trace the parallels.

Figure 26. Reading Log Prompts.

8. After reading this far, what more do you hope to learn about what these characters plan to do, what they think, feel, believe, or what happens to them?

9. Do you ever wish that your own life or the people you know were more like the ones in the story you're reading? In what ways would you like the real world to be more like the world of your book?

10. With what characters do you identify most closely or feel the most sympathy? What is it about these characters that makes you feel this way?

11. How much do you personally agree or disagree with the way various characters think and act and the kinds of beliefs and values they hold? Where do you differ and why?

12. What issues in this story are similar to real-life issues that you've thought about or had some kind of experience with? How has the story clarified or confused your views on any of these issues?

13. What characters and situations in the story remind you of people and situations in your own life? How are they similar and how do they differ?

14. How did the characters or events in this book remind you of characters or events in other books you've read or movies or television shows you've seen? Do you prefer one of these treatments over the others? If so, why?

15. Write a dialogue between yourself and the character you would most like to meet and talk with. Do the same with one you would not want to meet.

16. Write a mini-description of a particular scene or character using single words only, no phrases or sentences.

17. Choose an incident that happens to a character and exaggerate it in the telling. Make it into a tall tale.

18. Choose a word or phrase that strikes you and complete a cluster/vignette.

19. Draw a map of a particular chapter or scene.

20. Ask a series of questions provoked by the story, questions you can't answer.

21. Write a letter to the author.

22. Describe what you hope to remember about this story ten years from now.

Figure 26 *continued.*

4 Using Computers across Disciplines

For the more adventurous, those who would like to initiate cross-disciplinary work with computers, I have included some sample lessons developed by colleagues at Woodinville High School. The best advice I can give you concerning interdisciplinary work is plan and plan some more.

Sample Lesson 1: Math Analysis

This lesson was developed by Holly Runyan, a colleague of mine at Woodinville High School. Students actually wrote a proposal, graphed it, and even drew or designed the scale model. The librarians rated the proposals and awarded the contract to the mock company that submitted the most convincing, thorough, and accurate proposal. Because there is not one right solution to this kind of problem, I think Holly's scenario is exquisite, exemplifying problem solving within and without her discipline:

Rational Function—Least Cost Expediting

The town of Woodinville has decided to build a huge swimming pool complex and is accepting bids on the job. You and your partner own a large contracting outfit. Your statistics department has just computed the equation:

$$C(t) = \frac{t^2 + 25t + 160}{2t - 2}$$

that models the amount of money in millions that you should charge for the job as a function of time in months. (They derived this equation from data collected on other similar jobs, taking into consideration the current cost of living. Thus, C = the amount in millions of your bid, to be determined by inserting the time [t] in months into the equation.)

Your job is to submit your company's bid. Your bid should include the cost to the town of Woodinville and the estimated completion date.

Sample Lesson 2: Biology

Fred Dahlem uses the computer lab to help his sophomores learn biology. Conceptually, what his classes did was use writing-across-the-curriculum procedures to learn the subject. Each week, students came to the lab to write a summary of the chapter they had read the week before. Students were divided into groups, and each group was responsible for a section of the biology chapter. Students wrote down the objectives of their sections (taken from an objective sheet prepared by their teacher), followed by summaries of those sections.

After writing about their sections, students saved their work in a class folder everyone had access to over the network. Other students in the class then copied, saved, and printed what each group wrote. At home that evening, students read over what they had copied and checked it against the entire chapter. What follows are the procedures students were asked to use for one of the chapters.

Chapter 3 Objectives

Log-on

Boot-up program

Go to Classes folder on Storage file server
   Open Dahlem
   Open Period 1 or 2
   Begin NEW file

Type your objective number and the first line or lines from the objective sheet.

Now type your objective summary. Be sure to include all vocabulary that applies. Make each vocabulary word bold. When you finish, go to Save As . . . , and use the following format to name and save your file:
   Your initials-objective number-period number. Before quitting the program, retrieve the other objective summaries for this chapter, copy them to your file, and print them out.

Prepare your workstation for the next class.

Sample Lesson 3: Math, Art, English Project

Concerned that the bare white walls of her classroom helped to project the idea that mathematics is inherently a dull subject, Holly Runyan came up with a way to transform those walls with student-painted murals reflecting various aspects of mathematics. Her lesson is interdisciplinary because it combines mathematics, art, and English. Although Holly did not use computers in her classroom, this lesson can easily be adapted to include a computer component.

Students in Holly's Accelerated Algebra II/Trigonometry class were asked to do research in the history of mathematics. She divided her students into groups of three, and each group was assigned a specific topic. Each group researched its topic and then produced a drawing representing the essential element(s) of that topic. Then students were asked to write a composition that explained their drawings. This part of the lesson took about two weeks.

Holly had her students make transparencies of their drawings. Then she used an overhead projector to project the drawings on the walls of her classroom. With brushes borrowed from the school's art department, Holly's students used the projected drawings as guides to paint their drawings onto the walls of the classroom. Students from other classes volunteered to help with this part of the project, cutting down on the time involved. Woodinville High School now has three murals: The History of Mathematics, The History of Computer Science, and A Gallery of Famous Problems.

Computers could easily be integrated into this lesson. After researching their topics, students could easily create their pictures using a painting program such as SuperPaint. In addition, students could use the computers to compose, edit, and print out their essays explaining their drawings. Teachers could use a PC viewer to project the drawings onto the walls of their classrooms if they wanted to have their students create a painted mural as Holly's students did. The students' drawings and accompanying essays could also be collected and published in a book of student writing if painting on the walls is not an option.

This activity offers a number of possibilities. Mathematics teachers who choose to use this lesson might ask fellow teachers from their school's art or English departments to give presentations to their classes before beginning this activity. English teachers who adapt this lesson for use in their own classrooms have the same option. This would be an excellent activity for the end of the school year, when students are often less attentive to their studies than to thoughts of summer vacation.

Sample Lesson 4: Literary Arts Magazine

This is an ongoing project I have supervised for the last three years. Students from all departments do quite a bit of writing, and we publish student and teacher artwork, nonfiction, and fiction. Every year, two students design the cover art and edit the literary arts magazine. The editors use Pagemaker (a powerful desktop publishing program) to lay out the magazine text and a flatbed scanner to digitize student art work. As the art department becomes more comfortable with SuperPaint, we are beginning to see computer-generated art as well.

Students submit their work to a student editor via the network. I have created a drop folder on the network, so students can make submissions simply by dragging their files into the drop folder called Lit Mag. The editor and the LAN administrator are the only people who have access to the drop folder. Once a student submits a file to the Lit Mag folder, it cannot be removed, just like mailing a letter. The editor of the magazine checks the drop folder and then reviews submissions. For students who submit typed manuscripts, the literary arts magazine editors either scan these submissions with Omnipage or have someone enter the manuscripts into the computer using Microsoft Works. The word-processed text is then imported and placed in a Pagemaker magazine template designed by students.

The editors then send the final laser-printed magazine to the district print shop, where it is duplicated and bound.

Sample Lesson 5: Biology—The Aunt Gladys Letter

This project comes from the Lake Washington High School science department. A few years ago, one of their teachers spent the day interviewing me about how to set up a networked lab, and, as a reward, the biology teachers sent me this lesson. It's a fine example of a writing-across-the-curriculum lesson.

> You have just received a letter from your Aunt Gladys, who "has heard such wonderful things about you." Both Aunt Gladys and Uncle Wilbur have insatiable curiosity. She is somehow under the impression that because you are taking biology you know the answers to just about all of life's mysteries. Here is the end of the letter:
>
> > . . . and so Uncle Wilbur's foot is better now. Anyway, honey, I do hope things are well with you. I've heard such wonderful things about you. Which reminds me; there's something I've been meaning to ask you . . .
> >
> > (Insert your question here)
> >
> > Now, remember, I'm getting along in years and your uncle and I haven't had the decent education you're getting. So when you write back you make sure to explain it in a way we can understand. Give my love to all.
> >
> > Love and Kisses,
Aunt Gladys and Uncle Wilbur
>
> That was the letter. You will choose a question at random out of a selection made up for you. Your assignment is to write Aunt

Gladys back in the form of a letter. Your letter must answer the question in a clear and concise manner. You must also cite at least two references which answer the question directly and *"expert witnesses" (such as another teacher or knowledgeable person) do not count as references.* Also, the letter should be no more than two pages. Drawings or illustrations that help to explain the question are supplemental, but are nonetheless encouraged. We don't want to bore Aunt Gladys. Have fun!

1. I was reading about the salmon runs, and I was wondering how those salmon find their way back to the same stream they were born in. How do they recognize it?

2. I saw this big flock of birds flying south for the winter, and I was wondering how birds can find their way back to the same place year after year. I know that many birds migrate out over the ocean, so they can't be navigating by sight alone.

3. Is it true that viruses, like colds and flu, are more frequent in winter? If that's true, why?

4. During the last heat wave, Great-Aunt Yolanda was visiting, and Uncle Wilbur said, "It sure is hot." Great-Aunt Yolanda said, "It isn't the heat, it's the humidity." And I got to wondering, why does the humidity make it feel hotter?

5. The last time I got sick, I ran a fever of 103 degrees. I was wondering—why do you get a fever when you are sick? What purpose does it serve?

6. I was watching one of those Marlin Perkins shows about sharks, and he said that sharks will attack a metal boat, but they usually won't attack a wooden one, unless they're provoked. Why?

7. I was looking at a PBS special about elephants, and I thought: why aren't there insects that big? It seems like all of the big animals are mammals. Why not insects? Or worms?

8. I have some flowers in the garden that are open in the day and closed at night and others that are closed during the day and open at night. Why do they do this?

9. Why do some people have dark skin and others have light skin? Is there any benefit of one or the other?

10. I was watching the news, and they found the skeleton of someone who'd been murdered. The coroner looked at it and could tell just from the skeleton that the person was Asian. How did the coroner know? What kinds of differences are there between skeletons that would let you know what race the person belonged to?

11. I was watching a robin in my front yard, and I wondered how they find worms? Do they feel them, or hear them, or is it something else?

12. Cousin Elwood just started raising rabbits, and he was telling me that sometimes a pregnant rabbit will absorb the babies back into her body and not be pregnant anymore. Why does this happen, and how?

13. I know that plants grow from seeds, and I suddenly wondered: how do they get seedless oranges? If they don't have seeds, how do they grow new orange plants? And where did the first one come from?

14. Cousin Elmer John just bought a purebred Doberman, and it turned out to have some kind of hip disease. My neighbor Veronica Shmeltz' purebred St. Bernard had the same problem, and so did Barney Harbottle's purebred German Shepherd. Is this a coincidence? If not, what is the disease, and why do purebred dogs get it?

15. I've heard of several people here in town that have hemophilia, and they're all men. My neighbor says that only men get hemophilia. Is this true? If so, why?

16. The last time I bought a carton of milk, it was already sour when I opened it. Why does milk thicken when it sours? And also, how is ordinary sour milk different from sour cream and yogurt?

17. Well, you know how much I love my garden, and it suddenly struck me as odd how all the plants know when to flower. Daffodils always flower in early spring, marigolds in early summer, asters in midsummer, and so on. Every year they flower at the same time as they did the year before. So, I thought I'd ask you, how do plants know to flower at the right time?

18. I was just thinking about when my feet fall asleep, and I wondered what causes that. Also, why do you get that "pins-and-needles" sensation afterwards?

19. It's been pretty cold lately, and whenever it's cold I get goosebumps. Suddenly, I started wondering: what *are* goose-bumps? Why do you get them when you're cold?

20. Cousin Elmer John just had to go to the doctor because he stepped on a nail, and the doctor gave him a tetanus shot. And I wondered, how do shots work? Why does getting a shot give you immunity against disease? Does the shot for a viral disease differ from a shot for a bacterial disease? Why haven't doctors been able to make a shot for colds?

Sample Lesson 6: History Magazine

The I-Search Paper is a good activity for encouraging students to investigate any issue important to them. In a history class, there are many avenues students might pursue, so I will narrow the options in this particular lesson, showing primarily how students might create a magazine that incorporates the features of an integrated application such as Microsoft Works.

Tell students that the class is going to publish a historical magazine that delves into a time period or theme they have been studying. Their magazine should include at least the following: features, commentary, music, movie or book reviews, and reports about business and science. Students will also want to create advertisements.

Ask students to bring several current magazines to class, and spend a class session examining the design of each one. Note each magazine's layout—the cover design, the table of contents, how text and graphics are used to highlight articles, the placement of advertise-ments, and how columns and headlines are used to separate text. Talk about the kind of articles each magazine prints, their length, and where they are placed on the page and within the magazine. If possible, the teacher should bring in samples of magazines from the period being studied so students can see how designs have changed over the years.

Because creating a magazine takes a lot of work, I would divide the project responsibilities. Divide the students into groups, making each group responsible for one of the categories mentioned above. In addition, a copy-editing team will be needed to proofread articles, and several individuals competent with computers (even if they have not

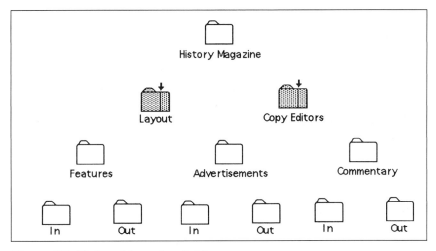

Figure 27. History Magazine Folder.

used a desktop publishing program) should act as layout editors. Their primary responsibility will be design consistency. Two more students will have to act as managing editors. Their job is to accept or reject story ideas and set deadlines. The students chosen as managing editors should be well-liked or strong, because they will be pressured to accept incomplete or poor work. This problem can be avoided by assigning a managing team that, through consensus, decides what is acceptable work and what is not. Once roles and groups are established, students can begin researching and writing articles.

One way to make this project more realistic is to use a networked lab to establish drop folders, creating the effect of a publishing house. Even in the smallest presses, staff writers post their work over a network using a form of electronic mail, and students can do the same thing in a networked computer lab. Make several drop folders within the project folder and give access to these folders to the individuals who are responsible for each department. The folders might look like Figure 27.

The gray folders with an arrow over them are drop folders in which reporters and artists submit their work. The managing editors or department heads have access to these folders, and their roles are to review the work and accept it, reject it, or request revisions.

Inside the layout folder, editors could have To Do, To Print, and Template folders. Work accepted by managing editors would be dropped into the To Do folder. Accepted work, whether prose or artwork, would be laid out on the template created with a desktop publishing application. This template (or templates) would be stored in the Template folder.

Finished pages would be copied to the To Print folder. To keep the entire magazine staff (i.e., the class) informed of their progress, galleys should be printed periodically and posted on the writing wall.

Reporters will also need a folder where they can save their work in progress. Figure 27 also shows three department folders: Features, Advertisements, and Commentary. Each of these folders contains In and Out folders. Reporters can save unfinished work inside the In folder, and when they are ready to show it to their department head, the file can be copied to the Out folder. Department editors check the Out folder, reading what reporters have submitted, passing on accepted work to the managing editors, and conferencing with reporters whose writing has not been accepted.

All of this may sound complicated, but it isn't. Sit down with scratch paper and sketch out the departments. Afterward, decide which departments need drop folders and then ask the LAN administrator to create them. If your students have not used the network, take them to the computer lab and demonstrate how files are copied to a drop folder and where files should be saved.

Encourage students to experiment with clip art and line, bar, and pie charts. Show students how they can use graphics and charts to recast information. If your school has a scanner, advertisements from the period your students have chosen to write about can be digitized and adapted using a drawing program. For example, if the time period is 1940–45, students might scan a photocopy of an Uncle Sam recruiting poster and a Campbell's Soup ad. Together these two ads create a new advertisement that tells the reader "Uncle Sam wants you to eat Campbell's Tomato Soup." The possibilities are limited only by time and imagination.

Again, bear in mind that students may care more about how the magazine looks than about what it says, especially if it is laser printed. The teacher (editor-in-chief), department editors, and managing editors will have to demand quality writing and in-depth research from their contributors. Students need to fulfill these goals before they submit work to a drop folder. Set several writing group times where department members can meet in the classroom to examine each other's work. I would also make transparencies of good work so the entire class can see what is being done by their peers. You might also create a writing wall dedicated to work students think is ready for publication. Before submitting a piece to a drop folder, students might first post their pieces for comments.

Projects of this magnitude have a way of taking on a life of their own; that's the good and bad news. As their teacher, you will find students immersed in the subject you love and that's good. You will also find the magazine, like a piranha, devouring time; that's the bad news. I suggest starting small or saving this kind of project for the last six weeks of the year, because it serves as a fine review.

Sample Lesson 7: History—Wagon Train 1848

Unlike the other sample lessons in this section, Wagon Train 1848* is a simulation developed specifically for a networked lab. The simulation is rich with cross-curricular connections. It helps students develop and practice communication, cooperative-learning, and problem-solving skills. It does much more than that as well, and the handbook that comes with the MECC program provides a variety of activities that can be used as is or employed as touchstones to spark the imagination.

Wagon Train 1848 takes users on a simulated journey across the Oregon Trail. This is an expanded version of MECC's Oregon Trail, a stand-alone program. Basically, the goal is to make the challenging journey from Independence, Missouri, to The Dalles, Oregon. One of the temptations of using this simulation is that students stress the software's game aspect. Because they have a Nintendo mentality, students want to outscore everyone and earn a spot at the top of the "Wagon Train List of Legends." Teachers will want to focus on transcending the game, helping students solve problems they will encounter along the way.

Real learning occurs when students begin seeing their wagon, and the members in it, as a vital part of the entire train. Students must negotiate within their own wagon and among other wagons as they encounter difficulties along the way. Of course, it is a lot easier to go it alone, but because this simulation is networked, it demands group problem solving. For example, the first group decision the wagon train will have to make is what kind of government they want. There are two types presented in the simulation: Council and Captain. If they select the Council option, all decisions made afterward are voted on and the majority rules. If they select the Captain option, the wagon train members select one person to lead the train. The Captain may make unilateral decisions or call for a vote. Both choices, however, allow for dissenting voices. And, as in all negotiated situations, the group can be swayed and a new form of government can be chosen.

---

* Wagon Train 1848 order inquiries can be mailed to MECC, 3490 Lexington Avenue North, St. Paul, Minnesota 55126-3551.

Obviously, the kind of leadership selected sets the tone that influences the journey.

Let me explain how Kathy Marion used the simulation with six groups of twelve seventh graders. What follows should show how Wagon Train 1848 can be adapted. Kathy chose this program because she knew it was nonthreatening and fun. Furthermore, it would help her encourage her students to work as a team to achieve a common goal. The first thing she did was to circle-up chairs in the computer lab, and, as their wagon master, provide the necessary simulation background followed by a discussion of the kind of government students would be voting on. This discussion allowed students time to think through the pros and cons of the two different forms of leadership. She then instructed wagons to "head 'em out." Students went to their computers, identified the members of their wagons, selected their professions, and bought supplies. Even this initial task required conversation, because students needed to negotiate which professions would best benefit the wagons on their journey.

When all twelve wagons were ready to travel the trail, they had to decide what form of government the train would use. Students were presented with an on-screen ballot and each wagon voted. And then the journey began.

This is where the simulation got interesting. As the wagon train continued its journey, students wanted to change the pace of the trip. However, depending on the kind of government they had chosen, a community vote had to be cast or the Captain had to decide for the train. For example, one wagon might decide it wanted to stop so they could go hunting. If students selected a Council government, the wagon put their idea to a vote and hoped the majority of the train agreed. Now, if disagreement occurred, the individuals representing a wagon could state their opinion in an attempt to sway the whole train. That was when a rationale was forwarded and reasons mustered.

Let's say the train agreed to stop and hunt. What students saw was an arcade-type game where they shot wildlife such as bison, elk, antelope, fox, bear, and rabbits. The first time Kathy's class voted to hunt, she incredulously watched her students go on a shooting spree. Instead of thinking about the scenario, students shot to beat the clock, seeing how many animals they could kill before time ran out. Although this was not a part of Wagon Train 1848, she circled-up her students so they could talk about what had transpired. Through guided questioning, students realized that food was wasted. One wagon killed 1,200 pounds of meat, even though it could only carry 200. The next time they went on a hunt, students killed only the game that they needed to survive. Students would not have stopped to think about the consequences of their actions during that first hunt if Kathy hadn't interrupted the simulation. They weren't hunting to survive; they were playing a game. The circle-up discussion added a new dimension to the simulation for these students. They began seeing the simulation as an authentic journey.

Students will learn many more valuable lessons along the trail, provided time is set aside to talk face-to-face about the day's adventures. Even though the simulation is designed solely for electronic communication over a network, Kathy found that her students needed to circle-up before and after each leg of the journey, because students learned more about negotiation, compassion, and experimentation through this human connection and interaction.

The Wagon Train 1848 handbook provides elaborate activities that can extend the simulation, helping students see beyond the game. This is a potentially rich and powerful program provided it is viewed as more than a game.

Afterword

There is a lot of information in this book, and I hope you aren't overwhelmed. My intention is to provoke some thought and get beginners started. The book is not an encyclopedia for technology, and that's why I have purposefully avoided talking about new software such as Quicktime or multimedia technology. I feel that the bridges our students build between individuals and groups are most important. You are the curricular expert, so I encourage you to use what is appropriate for your context and the individuals you teach.

My focus is on my students, helping them think about and articulate issues important to them. Because I care more about what is between my students' ears than the machine on the desk, I focus less on how something looks and more on what it means.

Our work is with whole people, not talking heads, not clicking fingers, not smiling screens. Today, every teacher's biggest challenge is imagining uses of technology that tap the potential in students, using what is discovered to help students reshape and take control of their world. Although writing and thinking with computers allows us to begin and extend conversations over time and distance, we should remember our work is with other human beings, not other machines. I invite your comments about how you have adapted or extended the lessons in this book. You can write me at 1819 North 48th Street, Seattle, Washington 98103.

Appendix: Learning Log Procedures

The learning log is simply a spiral notebook. What makes it different is how it is used. It is a place where students experiment with thinking about course material, and it is the cornerstone of my classes. What comes out of this preliminary thinking influences what we will read, write, and discuss as the class unfolds.

It is crucial that students think of the learning log as a safe place to think through writing; therefore, I never read it or collect it for any reason. However, anything in the learning log is potentially public domain, so students are asked not to reveal secrets. About every three weeks, I set aside a few minutes for a quick check of the learning logs—that is, students show me they have all the assigned entries and are keeping a record of their mechanical errors. I enter a check in my grade book if all entries are included, labeled, and dated.

To maintain the spirit of the learning log, most of the writing in it is done in class. I encourage students to write fast, allowing their hands to surprise them. They are trying to extend and experiment with ideas, instead of trying to say something "right."

Every learning log entry should include the following:

- the date for every entry
- a title for every entry (e.g., focused write, speculative starter #1, etc.)

Divide the learning log into two categories:

- assigned writing
- personal editing notes

Assigned Writing

Assigned writes are those entries I have developed. Assigned writes get at a particular concept or require a particular skill. Assigned writes are developed to get students to think about an idea or rehearse skills.

Personal Editing Notes

Teaching the mechanical processes of language should be done in a meaningful context. The following recording procedure replaces drill and practice work sheets. If this record is maintained consistently, students can monitor their own progress. Students should reserve about five pages at the end of their learning logs for this activity. Make sure students record only chronic problems.

Personal Editing Notes Procedures

1. Write down persistent errors you or the teacher have identified.
2. Copy the sentence and underline the error in it.
3. Use classroom references, find the applicable rule, and note it in the learning log.
4. Rewrite your sentences in accordance with the rule.
5. Maintain an ongoing record of persistent grammatical errors throughout the year.

Suggested Record Form

Date	Personal Error	Rule	Correction
11/12	*There* house is bigger than our house.	Possessive Pronoun	*Their* house is bigger than our house.

After a piece of writing is complete, when it is ready to go public, it is time to edit for grammar, spelling, and punctuation, using the above procedures. The following list is a guide to the most common mechanical errors most developing writers make.

Common Mechanical Errors

1. subject-verb agreement
2. appropriate capitalization
3. appropriate end punctuation
4. grade-level comma usage
5. sentence construction
   fragments
   run-ons
   overreliance on linking verbs
6. dialogue punctuation: quotation marks and commas
7. spelling
8. homophones (e.g., there/their/they're and to/too/two)

Works Cited

Berke, J. (1976). *Twenty questions for the writer.* New York: Harcourt, Brace Jovanovich.

Dillard, A. (1986). Living Like Weasels. In R. DiYanni (Ed.), *Literature: Reading fiction, poetry, drama, and the essay.* (pp. 1449–53). New York: Random House.

Elbow, P. (1973). *Writing without teachers.* New York: Oxford University Press.

Gere, A. R. (Ed.). (1985). *Roots in the sawdust.* Urbana, IL: National Council of Teachers of English.

Irmscher, W. (1981). *The Holt guide to English: A comprehensive handbook of rhetoric, language, and literature* (3rd ed.). New York: Holt, Rinehart, Winston.

Killgallon, D. (1984). *Sentence composing 11.* New Jersey: Boynton/Cook.

Marcus, S. (1991). Invisible Writing with a Computer: New Sources and Resources. In W. Wresch (Ed.), *The English classroom in the computer age: Thirty lesson plans* (pp. 9–13). Urbana, IL: National Council of Teachers of English.

McKenzie, J. (1984). Accordion writing—Expository composition with the word processor. *English Journal, 73*(5), 56–58.

Roethke, Theodore. (1980). Elegy for Jane. In F. Hodgins & K. Silverman (Eds.), *Adventures in American literature.* New York: Harcourt, Brace Jovanovich.

Wresch, W. (Ed.). (1984). *The computer in composition instruction: A writer's tool.* Urbana, IL: National Council of Teachers of English.

Wresch, W. (Ed.). (1991). *The English classroom in the computer age: Thirty lesson plans.* Urbana, IL: National Council of Teachers of English.

Wresch, W. (1985). *Writer's helper handbook.* Iowa City, IA: CONDUIT.

Resources for Teachers

As you develop and expand your thinking about the shape application-based curriculum might take at your school, consider the following resources:

Books

Collins, J. L. & Sommers, E. A. (Eds.). (1985). *Writing on-line: Using computers in the teaching of writing.* Upper Montclair, NJ: Boynton/Cook.

Cooper, C. R. & Odell, L. (1977). *Evaluating writing: Describing, measuring, judging.* Urbana, IL: National Council of Teachers of English.

Harper, D. O. & Stewart, J. H. (Eds.). (1983). *Run: Computer education.* Monterey, CA: Brooks/Cole.

Kirby, D. & Kuykendall, C. (1991). *Mind matters: Teaching for thinking.* New Hampshire: Boynton/Cook.

Rodrigues, D. & Rodrigues, R. J. (1986). *Teaching writing with a word processor, grades 7–13.* Urbana, IL: Educational Resources Information Center. (ERIC: ED 268 547).

Selfe, C. L. (1989). *Creating a computer-supported writing facility: A blueprint for action.* Urbana, IL: National Council of Teachers of English.

Selfe, C. L., Rodrigues, D., & Oates, W. R. (Eds.). (1989). *Computers in English and the language arts.* Urbana, IL: National Council of Teachers of English.

Wresch, W. (Ed.). (1984). *The computer in composition instruction: A writer's tool.* Urbana, IL: National Council of Teachers of English.

Wresch, W. (Ed.). (1991). *The English classroom in the computer age: Thirty lesson plans.* Urbana, IL: National Council of Teachers of English.

Young, R. E., Becker, A. L., & Pike, K. L. (1970). *Rhetoric: Discovery and change.* New York: Harcourt, Brace & World.

Journal Articles

Carroll, J. A. (1991). Drawing into meaning: A powerful writing tool. *English Journal,* 80(6), 34–38.

Kreidler, W. J. (1984). Teaching computer ethics. *Electronic Learning,* 3(4), 54–57.

Periodicals

The Assembly on Computers in English Newsletter
c/o Pam Farrell, ACE Treasurer
The McCallie School
2850 McCallie Avenue
Chattanooga, Tennessee 37404

The Computing Teacher
International Society for Technology in Education
1787 Agate Street
Eugene, Oregon 97403-1923

MacUser
P.O. Box 56986
Boulder, Colorado 80322

The Writing Notebook
P.O. Box 1268
Eugene, Oregon 97440

Catalogs

Conduit English Software	1-800-365-9774
EduCorp	1-800-843-9497
Humanities Software	1-800-245-6737
MacConnection	1-800-334-4444
MacWareHouse	1-800-255-6227